You are holding a prophetic book that is
challenging. This step-by-step exposé is
socio-political justice that must not go
extreme pain be in vain.

Alexander F. Venter – Pastor, Vineyard Christian Fellowship, Johannesburg

Ben Freeth is a man of strong Christian faith – full of love and forgiveness
for those who have brought great suffering upon him and his family. In
this book, he looks at what it means to be persecuted for one's faith and
the times when God calls upon the church to make a stand. It is a reminder
that our faith is nothing if we are not prepared to give everything.

*Revd Nicky Gumbel, pioneer of Alpha and Vicar of Holy Trinity Brompton
Church in London*

This book is a very courageous endeavour to bring to light the terrible
injustices in Zimbabwe. It appeals to all Christian people to be faithful to
what God is asking us to do: to stand for truth and not to forget justice,
mercy, and faithfulness. I believe this book will be used mightily. It is a
compelling read.

*General the Lord Dannatt GCB CBE MC DL, Chief of the General Staff
2006-2009*

A must read for Christians who take Jesus at his word, believing we must
be "salt" and "light" in an unjust world.

Archbishop Emeritus of Cape Town, Desmond Tutu

Ben Freeth raises the fundamental question of, what would Christ do in
the face of gross injustice and extreme violations of human rights? His
exploration of his faith, as the wellspring of his values, shows that the
answer lies within the reach of us all.

Alice Mogwe, Director, Ditshwanelo–The Botswana Centre for Human Rights

"In the vehicle of a brutal dictatorship, fear is the petrol that keeps the
engine going," writes Ben Freeth. He calls on the church to fulfil its God-
ordained role to challenge injustice and unrighteousness, and individuals
to rally behind the truth so that the curtain of lies and deception that keep
ruthless regimes in power can be torn down.

Sir Ranulph Fiennes, British explorer and author

It is a long, long road, the road to justice and peace in Zimbabwe. Ben
Freeth's personal story of standing up to violence and intimidation by the
Mugabe regime in Zimbabwe sets us a challenge – one way or another
wherever we face oppression, we must all take our stand. Black and white
together, we must stand for justice, and pray for peace. Love and justice
must pervade our environment if we are to embrace peace.

Dr John Sentamu, Archbishop of York

Jesus invaded Ben's horror story with astonishing grace. He stirs us to passion, longing, and hope. May his testimony persuade many to pursue truth and justice in our own lands.

Jackie Pullinger MBE, founder of the St Stephen's Society, Hong Kong

This piece of work is an excellent account of what happens when rulers fail. It is done according to the one real test of a successful ruler, namely whether that ruler succeeded or failed his or her God-given calling to uphold true justice and to protect the lives, dignity and property of his or her subordinates.

Willie Spies, legal representative: AfriForum, South Africa

Ben Freeth MBE is a British-born Zimbabwean farmer who successfully sued Mugabe in an international court in 2008. Since winning the suit he has been harassed and his farm burnt to the ground. His family's story was told in a compelling and award-winning documentary, Mugabe and the White African (2009), and subsequently in Ben's first book with the same title (2011).

WHEN GOVERNMENTS STUMBLE

LESSONS FROM ZIMBABWE'S PAST; HOPE IN AFRICA'S FUTURE

BEN FREETH
MBE

MONARCH
BOOKS

Oxford, UK & Grand Rapids, Michigan, USA

Published by Monarch Books
an imprint of
Lion Hudson plc
Wilkinson House, Jordan Hill Road,
Oxford OX2 8DR, England
Email: monarch@lionhudson.com
www.lionhudson.com/monarch

ISBN 978 0 85721 374 7
e-ISBN 978 0 85721 483 6

First edition 2013

Text acknowledgments
Every effort has been made to trace the original copyright holders where required.
In some cases this has proved impossible. We shall be happy to correct any such
omissions in future editions.
Scripture quotations taken from the Holy Bible, New International Version,
copyright © 1973, 1978, 1984 International Bible Society. Used by permission of
Hodder & Stoughton, a member of the Hodder Headline Group. All rights reserved.
'NIV' is a trademark of International Bible Society. UK trademark number 1448790.
Extracts (marked KJV) from The Authorized (King James) Version. Rights in the
Authorized Version are vested in the Crown. Reproduced by permission of the
Crown's patentee, Cambridge University Press.
pp. 48–49: Extract from *The Zimbabwean*, May 2012. Reprinted by kind permission
of *The Zimbabwean*, www.thezimbabwean.co.uk

Picture acknowledgments
p. 1: Time & Life Pictures/Getty (top); United States Holocaust Memorial Museum
(middle); Wiener Library/epa/Corbis (bottom)
p. 2: Corbis (top left); AP/TopFoto (top right); ITAR-TASS Photo Agency/Alamy
(bottom)
p. 3: Forum/UIG/The Bridgeman Art Library (top left); HMK/Release International
(top middle); World History Archive/TopFoto (top right); János Antal, ecumenical
officer (Reformed Church in Romania) (bottom)
p. 4: Royal Geographical Society, London, UK/The Bridgeman Art Library (top left);
Michael Graham-Stewart/The Bridgeman Art Library (top right); Eric Fick (bottom)
p. 5: Robin Hammond/Panos (top and middle); Anonymous for security reasons
(bottom)
p. 6: AP/Press Association (top and middle); Solidarity Peace Trust (bottom)
p. 7: Gallo Images/Reuters (top); Robin Hammond/Panos (middle); Ben Freeth
(bottom left); Anonymous for security reasons (bottom right)
p. 8: AP/Press Association (top); Peau D'ane supplied by Claire Freeth (bottom)

A catalogue record for this book is available from the British Library

Printed and bound in the UK, September 2013, LH26

Dedication

I would like to dedicate this book to all Christians who would take the courage to climb the mountain of the truth in days of persecution to come, and continue to stand on the top of it – however exposed or lonely a place it may appear to be.

CONTENTS

ACKNOWLEDGMENTS

Everyone who has helped with this book and in the often precarious stand for truth against the deceit and violence of evil men in authority knows who they are. My family and my friends and those who have supported the Mike Campbell Foundation have been absolutely amazing. May God bless you and make his face shine upon you, and may you be inspired to carry on standing for the truth. Thank you from the bottom of my heart.

FOREWORD

Ben Freeth's incredible Christian faith, courageous fight for the rule of law, ability to face fear, and his passion for his home country of Zimbabwe are qualities that I so admire in this humble yet determined man.

Taking on a dictator is no mean feat and he has had countless close shaves, notably the abduction and torture that almost cost his life and later took the life of his father-in-law, Mike Campbell.

When Governments Stumble is a fascinating and thought-provoking book that challenges people's tendency throughout the ages to avoid confronting tyranny because the backlash is likely to be so brutal.

"As Christians," he says, "I believe we have been led to fight for justice." For Ben, Mike, and the family, this involved taking on the Mugabe government in a court case that challenged the violent invasion of commercial farms across the country. Throughout their confrontation with the Mugabe regime they knew the dangers: "A man can defend himself and his family from armed robbers, but not from an entire government," he reasons.

Standing for justice under a dictatorship is the Mount Everest of faith. When law and order are stripped away – along with your home, livelihood, and possessions – you can only depend on God. This has been the case for people throughout Zimbabwe who were believed to pose a threat to the regime, including opposition party supporters, farm workers, and the urban and rural poor.

A mountain of faith is needed when the threat of an overcrowded, lice- and death-infested prison hangs over you because you have the temerity to stand against injustice, as so many brave innocents have discovered. Overcoming both moral fear and physical fear requires moral and physical courage.

Throughout the book Ben shows the relevance of Bible stories and parables – and their ethics – in modern-day life. He reminds us of godly men and women who overcame fear and defied the authorities, such as the midwives who refused to kill baby boys despite the explicit instructions of the Pharaoh, and Naboth, who refused to sell his vineyard, even under extreme duress.

Ben quotes Martin Luther King Jr: "No one really knows why they are alive until they know what they'd die for", and cites examples like Daniel in the lion's den and Shadrach, Meshach, and Abednego, who were thrown bound into a burning, fiery furnace by the Babylonian king, Nebuchadnezzar.

What is especially interesting in each case was the appearance of an angel. Shadrach, Meshach, and Abednego referred to the presence as a "fourth man" who rescued them unscathed, while Daniel reported that God had sent an angel who had shut the mouths of the lions. Ben gives modern-day examples in Zimbabwe of incredible angelic intervention and protection.

Sir Ernest Shackleton, in his book *South*, described his belief that an incorporeal being joined him and two others during the final leg of their long and traumatic march over the mountains and glaciers of South Georgia. "It seemed to me often that we were four, not three," he wrote. A study of cases involving adventurers reported that the largest group to have experienced phenomena of this nature involved climbers, with solo sailors and shipwreck survivors being the second most common group, followed by polar explorers.

Faced with tyrannical governments, Ben stresses that churches are compelled to speak out, be it against the persecution of the Jews by the Nazi regime, the oppression of the Polish people under Communism, or the Romanians under the dictatorship of Nicolae Ceaușescu. The world needs Christian men and women who are prepared to overcome their fear and to stand against injustice and persecution. He gives examples of church leaders whose remarkable courage helped to turn the tide of history.

Ben explains how attacks on property rights are attacks on man's fundamental freedom. And that the direct result of the abolition of property rights is that the land becomes a desolate waste and the people starve.

Revisiting British history, Ben explains how the Magna Carta of 1215 – the Great Charter of Liberties of England – came into being, giving power to the people and enshrining the right to due process in law. More than 400 years later, Christian-inspired enlightenment drove the Glorious Revolution of 1688, which led to the protection of property rights through the law. This resulted in the agricultural revolution through which Britain became the most efficient agricultural nation in the world at the time.

Ben also deals with the mystery of grace – the place where justice and forgiveness meet. He gives a powerful personal testimony of his journey to redemption, and wonders at the courage of brave friends who have risked their lives by walking in such amazing grace. "Yes, these are the risk takers who will advance my kingdom," Jesus said.

"Truth" is a powerful thread that runs throughout the book. When Christians stand courageously for truth and justice, whatever the circumstances, dictatorships will be overcome and extreme poverty will end. Ben challenges us all to stand up courageously and to walk in faith to help those with no voice to overcome tyrannical rule. Through this we can become the voices for truth in the fight for justice and freedom in our world.

BEAR GRYLLS

WOULD WE IGNORE?

I wrote these lyrics to the tune of "Jerusalem" after reading of the church on the railway line to Auschwitz where, when the death trains went by with cargos of Jews destined for the gas chambers, the congregants simply decided to drown out the desperate cries for help by singing their hymns louder…

Would we ignore the cries of pain,
As death trains went on screaming by?
Would we as Christians let them go –
Slaves to fear and Satan's lie?

And would we turn our heads away?
And sing our hymns mechanically?
And would we let ungodly laws,
Entrench themselves to make us fall?

What can we do? What can we say?
How can we breathe life back at all?
How should we fight? How should we pray?
To conquer fear – that is our call.

To overcome, we need to trust,
And know the hand that holds us high.
And be cleansed by Jesus' blood,
And speak out, unafraid to die!

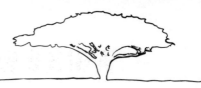

The lie is burnt, the sword is smelted.
In love and truth the fire was made.
The mountain shakes! God's finger blazes!
The light flares up! The price is paid!

Love conquers fear – makes blind men see.
We speak out and evil flees.
We break the yoke, set captives free,
Ever standing – in victory!

So let us stand, undaunted, strong.
Let's not be cowed by evil men.
Like Stephen, with heaven's song!
Like Daniel, brave in lions' den!

I count as dross my earthly things,
My shroud is bare, no pockets there.
My life is short, the death bell rings –
Heaven awaits, the King of Kings!

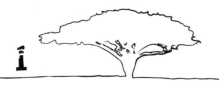

A DEPARTURE FROM THE RULE OF LAW AND JUSTICE IN ZIMBABWE

They overcame him by the blood of the Lamb and by the word of their testimony; they did not love their lives so much as to shrink from death. (Revelation 12:11)

They didn't stand a chance.

It was a quiet Sunday afternoon. My parents-in-law, Mike and Angela Campbell, were busy feeding an orphaned calf when the Gilbert Moyo gang attacked without warning. They tore down the drive of the farm and immediately began beating Mike. Angela ran at them, screaming for them to stop – a 67-year-old against a gang of heavily armed young men. She was enveloped by sheer, violent evil. The men snapped her arm as if she were a small child then began beating her over the head. They continued to assault Mike brutally. Eventually, both were dragged a short distance away and roughly tied. Some of the gang urinated on them as they lay bleeding and broken in the dust.

I had received warning a short time before from some workers at another farm that Moyo's gang were on the rampage and on their way to us on Mount Carmel farm next. Moyo was ruthless. He knew no restraint and had carte blanche from the government to terrorize, beat, and rob people. He was authorized to do whatever was necessary to get us out of our homes. The other farm had been hit that morning and the workers had overheard the gang saying they were coming for us next. I had jumped in the pick-up and had sped over to the other side of the farm to warn Mike and Angela.

As I came around the corner I was greeted by two of the gang, brazenly wearing Mugabe T-shirts, with rifles pointed directly at my head. I couldn't see Mike or Angela anywhere, just the weapons. I jumped on the brakes, ducking under the dashboard to avoid being shot, and slammed the car into reverse, gearbox screaming, every fibre of my being focused on getting away. I stood on the brakes again, thrust the gear lever into first, and hit the accelerator. Wheels spun as I tried to turn around. I thought I was succeeding, gaining speed, into second gear... then a thug came from nowhere with a large rock, shattering my side window. I felt granite thudding into my head and I was down and dazed. Covered in glass and blood I kept my foot on the accelerator in a desperate attempt to continue my escape, but came to a sudden dead halt as I hit the mahogany tree on the edge of the driveway.

The pick-up door was yanked open and rough hands dragged me out. I resisted with every ounce of strength I could muster, but I was a rag doll in the hands of malevolent giants. The woollen jersey my grandmother had given me was ripped off, my shirt was torn open, my shoes were pulled off. The men threw me to the ground and began the vicious, systematic beating that ZANU-PF metes out to opponents of the ruling party. Instinctively I rolled onto my stomach, trying to curl up as rifle butts rained down on my head and body, accompanied by shouts of abuse. I lay writhing, hopelessly trying to defend myself against the blows, but was completely outnumbered and overpowered. They persisted until the last remnant of resistance was beaten out of me.

Semi-conscious, I was dragged through the dirt to where Mike and Angela lay. I will never forget the horror of seeing their bloody, broken bodies crumpled on the hard gravel. Mike was unconscious. Angela was stunned and in considerable pain, her face a mass of swollen bruises. Her arm hung awkwardly. They were tied with the inch-thick blue nylon rope I had seen hanging in Mike's workshop. The red earth around was stained redder still with their blood. I was too dazed to say anything.

I was tied and dumped next to them and we watched impotently as load after load of possessions were looted from Mike and Angela's house and carried past us to the waiting vehicles. I heard a series of shots. They were shooting out the tyres on my pick-up truck. I wondered whether we would live or die.

All around us the government's men chattered among themselves, each wearing the customary T-shirts bearing the president's face. Mugabe had been sworn back into power that afternoon following a bloody election campaign where Zimbabwe's people had been cowed into compliance by torture and the kind of brutality we were experiencing.

There were a lot more shots and then a hurried departure. They hauled us into Mike's truck, stealing that as well, and soon we were travelling at speed down pothole-ridden roads, feeling every jolt. Like Mike, I fell in and out of consciousness. I was dimly aware of more shooting, shouting, and confusion.

We arrived at the gang's base at Pickstone Mine, on the east side of Chegutu, in the cold and dark. Though it was cold enough for frost, they still poured buckets of freezing water over us – reputedly part of their indoctrination process. One had to be "baptized" into the dark spirits of the government's way of thinking.

I could see gang members milling around campfires. Most were young men, little more than boys. They were singing their revolutionary "Chimurenga" (war) songs. A number of them carried guns. They discharged rounds at will and took a particular delight in pointing them at us.

Gilbert Moyo and some of the other leaders of the torture base went off in one of the stolen vehicles – presumably to receive instructions from those higher up, to learn whether or not they were to kill us. Above, between the crowns of the trees, stars pricked the black velvet sky with pins of light. I thought back to perhaps the only other time in my life I had ever felt so utterly powerless…

I was in Grindelwald, Switzerland, with my father – a former captain of the British Ski Team and a Commonwealth Games gold medallist. I was sixteen then and Dad had given me the honour of being the first person to carve tracks down a beautiful, snow-smooth virgin slope. We had walked up to it, high on an alpine ridge, far off the beaten track. I launched myself over the cornice and landed with a loud whoop of joy on the steep slope of light, untracked powder that had fallen the night before.

In an instant, however, the flawless white slope cracked like crazy paving. Everywhere snaking cracks, which have been known to move quicker than the speed of sound, darted away from me and great slabs of packed snow rose on their ends all around me. I knew I had to straight line it – try to outrun the rapidly forming avalanche by skiing straight down this incredibly steep slope. Now another problem presented itself: it was −10 °C and the fresh powder was featherlight on the surface. The avalanche became airborne – the type that can move at more than 300 km per hour.

I gained speed fast, struggling to keep my balance as the snow beneath me rose like a tidal wave, but the avalanche was faster. My skis were plucked from me and I was catapulted down the rocky slope at the mercy of the relentless forces that had gathered in seconds to display a spectacle of awesome power.

I somersaulted over and over in a white fury of flying snow, unable to do anything but comply with the forces at work. I had no idea where I would end up or in what state. My father, lonely, up on the ridgeline, watched his son vanish into the white chaos that billowed up, exposing the brutal rock face underneath. At that moment he prayed. "Father, bring him back to me!"

I was suddenly struck by the thought that I had to "swim" for my life. Frantically, I began to kick my legs and throw my arms over and over, as if striking hard to stay on top of an ocean wave. I felt the avalanche slowing, coming to a halt and suddenly I was straitjacketed – no longer able to kick or move my arms. I was locked down, as though a concrete dumper had poured a ton of instant setting mix into a hole with me at the bottom. I had been rapidly, immovably fixed. The billions of feathered, tiny snowflakes that had fallen and settled the night before were now lying in a jumbled mass at the foot of the slope, with me buried among them. For a couple of glorious hours that morning, their magnificent, individual crystals had glittered like jewels in the mountain sun. Now there was only a dark, jagged rock face.

By his grace, God answered my father's prayer. As I thrust out with my arms, I'd hit the top of my stroke just as the avalanche ground to a halt. This undoubtedly saved my life. Two fingers of one hand were left exposed and able to move, just above the surface. Though I couldn't breathe with the hard-packed snow pressed against my mouth and nose, I was able to quickly gouge out the snow with my fingers and begin to move my hand. With some frantic scrabbling, I was gradually able to get some movement in my arm. Time stood still as my body screamed to break free. Eventually I managed to scrape the snow away from my face so that I could breathe at last. Several minutes later and I was digging myself out, gasping the free mountain air. I could see the forlorn figure of my father, picking his way down the rock face towards me as fast as he could.

The sharp frost of the Zimbabwean night snapped me away from my thoughts. I was freezing in shorts and my still-wet, ragged shirt. I stank of blood, sweat, and the thugs' urine. My head was throbbing constantly after the vicious beating. I didn't know it then, but the rifle butts had badly fractured my skull. I was nursing several broken ribs too, and ached all over.

I would later learn more about the events surrounding our beating and kidnap. Friends of ours, aware of the attack, had made reports to the local police, but at Chegutu police station they were refusing to act, responding with the usual indifference. In fact, after being bundled into one of the stolen vehicles, we had passed a police car along the quiet road about 6 km from the farm. It appeared that the police had been monitoring Moyo's progress, but as we flew past in our gangster convoy, guns bristling out of every window and random shots being fired, there was no question of the police intervening.

The policewoman in the Chegutu charge office had laughed at my wife, Laura, when she reported the abduction and beating of her elderly parents and husband that afternoon. Laura had to be restrained from slapping her. She too had had a traumatic afternoon, hurrying to gather the children and get them out of the house, along with our dogs and a few possessions, before the gang got there. She had heard the repeated gunshots at her parents' house on the other side of the farm where I had gone. She had no idea whether any of us were dead or alive.

Laura's escape route with our three children, my future sister-in-law, Grace, and my niece, Megan, had been miraculous. Laura and the children heard the shooting and, after Bruce told them to get out of our house, she loaded the dogs and a few possessions into the Ford Laser while Grace drove her car with the children in it. The Laser, at over twenty years old, is low to the ground. It was never designed for dirt tracks in the bush, but it was evident from all the shooting that Laura had to go out through the bush on the northern boundary rather than risk being shot at on the main road. Megan started crying.

"You mustn't cry, you must pray," Grace told her. The children prayed and Megs stopped crying.

When they got to the northern fence, neither Grace nor Laura had wire cutters. It is a tall game fence that Bruce had put up to try to protect the wildlife before it was all poached away. Laura said a prayer, and out of the bush walked a man with a dog. "The man had a lovely face," she told me later, "and the dog looked healthy and well fed." This was very unusual in a land where even the people are hungry. Laura had never seen the man before, and has never seen him or his dog since.

Laura briefly explained the situation to him. Without a word he pulled some wire cutters out of his back pocket and walked over to the fence. He cut through it and opened it out. As she and Grace drove through, he told them which tracks to take. They got to the police station without further incident.

Bruce, Laura's brother, had been alerted to the attack and arrived in time to try to trail us, but he had been shot at repeatedly. Several bullets missed his head by inches and he was forced to abandon the chase. At the station he showed the police the numerous bullet holes in his car, but still they refused to go out and arrest the government thugs and rescue us. Meanwhile, other friends had driven 30 km north to Selous, but the police there had also refused to do anything to help. At Kadoma, 40 km south, other friends were met with similar indifference. Laura had told the police that Gilbert Moyo would almost certainly have taken us to his torture base, located near Pickstone Mine, but it was clear that they had instructions from higher up not to go there. Our experience was like that of so many others. Government-sponsored criminals had committed thousands of similar crimes over the previous eight years. In our case, we also knew that the powers that be were making an example of us. Anyone daring to take on the president and having the temerity to pursue justice in the courts was committing a heinous crime and must be severely dealt with.

Moyo was well known to us as a government "untouchable". Police, from the lowest to the highest, refused to bring him to account. Earlier that day Moyo had looted Blake Nicolle's house, taken everything, and left the place bare. No doubt it was a reward for running a successful campaign for the president. Next he had moved on to Frank Trott on Twyford Farm, broken some of Frank's ribs, and put a gun to his head. I recognized the red pick-up that one of Moyo's men was driving as one stolen from Kobus Joubert – a farmer from just up the road. Moyo had slaughtered all the chickens and a sheep on the farm, stolen the farm diesel, and generally caused as much havoc as possible. Kobus had "connections" and managed to summon the senior police officer for the whole district to his farm. She negotiated with Moyo to leave Kobus alone, but still allowed him to drive away scot free in the stolen pick-up. Tragically, some time later Kobus was shot dead on his farm while in his bed.

The previous two months or so had seen Moyo and his gang involved in breaking down the doors of half a dozen other homesteads, mainly stealing weapons and causing widespread terror. During one such visit his gang had beaten Bruce and Nettie Rogers very badly. They'd received warning ahead of time that Moyo was on his way and alerted Chegutu police. Assistant Inspector Bepura from PISI – the feared Police Internal Security Intelligence – had said that he was not going to act, so the gang duly attacked at dusk and broke into the house. They lit fires on the open floors downstairs to try to force Bruce and Nettie to come down from upstairs where they were holding their ground. When they refused, they were fired upon at close range with a shotgun. Fortunately they were not hit, but Moyo used a human shield of farm workers to come up the stairs. Eventually, Bruce and Nettie agreed to vacate their home in peace. Moyo, however, captured them and beat them severely with iron bars, breaking vertebrae in Bruce's back, which gives him constant pain five years later. Bruce and Nettie would have been abducted, but for the miraculous arrival of the Kadoma police riot squad, who were finally persuaded to come to the scene. Although police intervention saved Bruce and Nettie's lives, Moyo and his gang were again allowed to drive away as free men to continue their violence. The Rogers family were left without a home or even a teaspoon to their name.

My first encounter with Moyo had been some years before all this, when he had been evicting James Ogden-Brown. James had been involved in assisting the opposition leader, Morgan Tsvangirai, giving him support during the election. To a dictator, any such support is a treasonable offence. Moyo broke into James's house and stole his guns before turning them on us who, at about four in the morning, had come to try to help James, his wife, and young children, who were under severe threat. In the familiar run of things, the police refused to come out to assist us because this was "political" and they had their orders. So we had decided to drive over to them ourselves to try to help. Moyo shot directly at us with the stolen firearms, hitting one of the vehicles. Diesel tanks were speared and hundreds of litres of diesel were either stolen or allowed to run into the ground. More than a hundred workers were suddenly without jobs. When the dust had settled and the police eventually arrived on the scene, they refused to arrest or even caution Moyo. In Zimbabwe, justice and the rule of law were being systematically demolished and everyone was suffering.

The founder of the International Justice Mission, Gary Haugen, identifies injustice occurring at the point at which "power is misused to take from others what God has given them, namely their life, dignity, liberty or the fruits of their love and labour".[1] Fundamentally, injustice is about the abuse of power. The seventh edition of the Oxford Dictionary defines justice as the "exercise of authority in maintenance of right". Justice is therefore the *right use* of power by those who possess it.

God is a God of justice. He has put laws in place in the universe that cannot be broken without severe consequences. The psalmist praises God, saying, "A sceptre of justice will be the sceptre of your kingdom" (Psalm 45:6).

The breakdown of the Zimbabwean justice system began when the police were instructed not to act against certain, specific crimes committed by specific people. Crimes committed against various sectors of the civilian population of Zimbabwe in the run-up to the election in 2000 were numerous and widespread. They were designed to bring terror, and they did. The opposition, in the form of the Movement for Democratic Change (MDC), was unable to campaign on the commercial farms. Meetings were not allowed. Perceived supporters were beaten and some were killed. Farm villages were burnt down. Land was invaded. Whenever police assistance was sought the answer was always the same: "We cannot assist because it is political."

Some people tried to resist the regime by taking court action against the State. Judgments were given in their favour, but still the police refused to obey them. The next phase in the breakdown was an attack on the judiciary and the appointment of new judges whose political loyalties to the president were proven beyond doubt. Any judges not loyal to the ruling party were harassed and threatened until they were forced to flee. In 2000 the police allowed the Supreme Court to be invaded while it was hearing a land case. The old guard of judges hearing the case had to retreat out of the back of the court. They became so fearful for their lives that they all took early retirement. Not a single white judge was able to remain in office.

Loyal black judges were given farms whose owners were forced to flee their homes. This was to cement their loyalty and to ensure that no judgments jeopardized the ruling party's grip on power. The government's control over the land, and more particularly the people who occupied that land, had to be complete because 70 per cent of voters lived in the rural areas making the rural vote crucial for Mugabe.

Next came the imposition of unjust laws. At the time of our abduction, despite the protection we had from the South African Development Community (SADC) Tribunal,[2] according to Zimbabwean law we were apparently committing a crime by farming our own land and living in our own home. The government created a law that effectively nationalized all white-owned farms, without offering any compensation for the land, and which criminalized any farmers or farm workers who remained in their homes without an offer letter, lease, or permit.[3] Refusing to leave was punishable by up to two years in prison.

To citizens of countries who live under a functioning justice system it is almost impossible to conceive what it is like when your government deliberately manipulates the rule of law to forcibly take away your home and life's work. It is difficult to imagine a police force that acts selectively or not at all when you need them to protect your property, even your life. Imagine a judiciary that refuses to make fair judgments; a parliament that makes laws designed to persecute you – that fly in the face of widely accepted human rights charters and contravene biblical principles.

A friend of ours, Heidi, going through the same turmoil as my family, described the process this way: it's like being thrust into a boxing ring with your hands tied behind your back. It is an appropriate analogy. Imagine yourself forced unwillingly into the ring with the heavyweight boxing champion of the world – and a few of his friends. You have never been in a boxing ring before. Suddenly the referee grabs your hands and ties them firmly behind your back. Any attempt to defend yourself or punch back is now impossible. In addition, the ring is in darkness apart from a bright spotlight focused on you, singling you out and at the same time partially blinding you. You have no idea where or when the next set of blows that assault you periodically will come from. The referee allows the fight to continue, round after round, until you are so bruised, sore, and fearful that you lose all capacity to think clearly about what you ought to do. You are told that if you break the rules by kicking, head butting, or biting your opponent, or if you call for help, the referee's punishment will be severe. In fact, if you resist at all your situation will become worse. If you protest, the referee penalizes you further and allows your opponent to punch "below the belt".

In such a situation what would you do? What *could* you do? I think there are three options: you try to dodge as many blows as you can until you are cornered and eventually knocked down;

you somehow wriggle free and run for your life; or, you pretend to join forces with your aggressor, consequently becoming one of his "friends" – part of the assault levied on the next innocent man to be pushed into the ring.

The "boxing ring" scenario is not uncommon in world history. It has been repeated many times and it will surface again. As Christians it is imperative we try to work out how to respond to the rule of tyranny, when the rule of law is usurped and dictators persecute the people they are supposed to protect.

Where Mike, Angela, and I were taken, out in the lonely veldt under the open sky, I knew that we could easily vanish without a trace. In Zimbabwe many thousands of people had disappeared before. It is a feature of life under a government so far away from godly principles. "Dead bodies don't speak," one of the gang had said.

I had never kept a gun in the house during the lawlessness because I knew it wouldn't have helped. It hadn't helped anyone else. This was not a war in which you were allowed to fight back. If you did, you would be killed like Martin Olds. When a gang had attacked Martin's home he had fired back, but they sent in reinforcements until eventually they got him. A few individuals, even with their large farm workforce, cannot win a shooting war against the might of an entire State with its guns, helicopters, tanks, and battalions of men. It was not that kind of war anyway. A man can defend himself and his family from armed robbers, but not from an entire government.

And yet, I was not afraid. Somehow God took away all fear. I was ready for whatever happened. In the chaos, pain, and extreme uncertainty of our situation, I prayed to God in the darkness, "If I am to die today, I'm ready. But if you still have things for me to do down here, then I am also ready."

When we decided to take on the full might of the State in a court case we had known it would be difficult. When Mike Campbell, my father-in-law, now lying groaning beside me, signed the court papers taking President Robert Mugabe to court, he had not done it with his eyes closed. He had known full well he could be signing his own death warrant. It was a momentous event for me. Tears had welled up in my eyes and run down my cheeks as he signed, because we all knew that the road ahead would be a road of many thorns. We could have carried on trying to "duck the blows"; we could have fled the farm; or we could have joined the appeasement men, the "collaborators consortium" as Mike used to call them – those who were paying protection money to the boxing champion and his men; hoping, like Churchill's proverbial feeders of crocodiles, that they would be the last to be eaten.

Our choice had been different. As Christians, I believe we had been led to fight for justice in the situation. We were convinced of the verse in Proverbs 29 that says, "the fear of man will prove to be a snare; but whoever trusts in the Lord is kept safe". It was fear of man that we had to guard against. Ungodly fear has always been a prime tool of Satan, working through ungodly governments. Lies and fear are what we must fight.

Moyo and the leaders of the torture base returned, having spoken to those higher up. They gave us the following ultimatum: "If you withdraw from the SADC Tribunal we will let you live." Unbeknown to us, our abduction had made headline news all over the world, appearing on most major TV networks. The Campbell case had already become well known internationally. It is not often an individual takes on a dictator in an international court. The timing of our abduction and beating, on the day that our adversary President Mugabe was being sworn back into power after beating the Zimbabwean people to a pulp, made the story into something huge.

Moyo wanted Mike to sign a bit of paper confirming our withdrawal from the courts. Mike was unconscious most of the time and they had smashed his hand so badly that he wouldn't have been able to sign anything. Angela's left arm hung awkwardly like the broken wing of a bird, but her right hand was working all right, so with guns trained on her she was made to sign the paper saying we would drop our court case against the government.

Within six months of Mugabe beginning his rule in 1980, he had signed a deal with North Korean President Kim II Sung for his soldiers to train what would become the "Fifth Brigade" – his own personal army. These were elite troops completely separate and distinct from the rest of the army. They had different codes, uniforms, radios, and equipment incompatible with that of other army units. As soon they were ready, the soldiers were sent down to Matabeleland in the south of the country, where the main minority tribe resided. Its men had been trained in Maoist totalitarian systems designed to break a civilian population.

A cordon was set around the area so that its people were unable to bring food back to their villages. Throughout history, deprivation of food has often been used as a weapon by the powers that be to starve the people into submission. Later, the Gukurahundi (or "early rain that blows away the chaff") massacres carried out by the Fifth Brigade would take place at the same time as President Mengistu of Ethiopia, a good friend of President Mugabe, was causing famine through a similar scorched earth policy. A document of Ethiopia's Council of Ministers read, "The people are the sea and the guerrillas are the fish swimming in the sea. Without the sea there will be no fish. We have to drain the sea."[4]

Mengistu "drained the sea", and hundreds of thousands of people perished – not so much from drought, as was claimed at the time, but from the Ethiopian government bringing people into such poverty and hunger that they became totally dependent on food aid for life. The great Band Aid rock concert was set up and pop stars sang to get people fed. They were bandaging the wound, but they never dealt with the people or system that had inflicted the wound and would continue to inflict more wounds.

In Zimbabwe the sea was drained too. The Fifth Brigade soldiers, commanded by Perence Shiri (current head of the

Zimbabwean Air Force) and Minister of State Security Emmerson Mnangagwa (current Minister of Defence), terrorized the people of Matabeleland. The brigade spread out, going from village to village. At each place, the villagers were brought together in compulsory meetings and intense fear generated – usually by making examples of people selected at random. Public torture and brutal killings were carried out. Events were orchestrated to ensure complete fear, so that political opposition could not continue to exist. The violence was indiscriminate. Victims included pregnant women, children, and even babies. The atrocities were mostly committed in the open, so that all the villagers could see the horror and be terribly afraid.

In 1997 two human rights organizations, the Legal Resources Foundation and the Catholic Commission for Justice and Peace, produced a report entitled "Breaking the Silence, Building True Peace".[5] The report speaks about the atrocities in some of the districts:

> *Five Brigade passed first through Tsholotsho, spreading out rapidly through Lupane and Nkayi, and their impact on all these communal areas was shocking. Within the space of six weeks more than 2,000 civilians had died, hundreds of homesteads had been burnt and thousands of civilians had been beaten. Most of the dead were killed in public executions involving between 1 and 12 people at a time.*
>
> *In late January 1983, 5 Brigade was deployed in Matabeleland North. Within weeks, its troops had murdered more than 2,000 civilians, beaten thousands more, and destroyed hundreds of homesteads. Their impact on the communities they passed through was shocking.*
>
> *Most of the dead were shot in public executions, often after being forced to dig their own graves in front of*

family and fellow villagers. The largest number of dead
in a single killing involved the deliberate shooting of 62
young men and women on the banks of the Cewale River,
Lupane, on 5 March 1983. Seven survived with gunshot
wounds, the other 55 died. Another way 5 Brigade killed
large groups of people was to burn them alive in huts.
This was done in Tsholotsho and also in Lupane.

At the same time as 5 Brigade was sent into the area,
the Government had introduced a strict curfew on the
region. This prevented anybody from entering or leaving
the area, banned all forms of transport, and prevented
movement in the region from dusk to dawn. A food
curfew was also in force with stores being closed. People
caught using bicycles or donkey carts were shot. No
journalists were allowed near the region. This situation
meant that it was very hard to get news of events out
of the region, and hard to judge the truth of the early
accounts. However, as some people managed to flee the
area, stories of the atrocities began to spread.

During these early weeks, 5 Brigade behaved in a way
that showed it had clearly been trained to target civilians.
Wherever troops went they would routinely round up
dozens, or even hundreds, of civilians and march them
at gunpoint to a central place, like a school or borehole.
There they would be forced to sing Shona songs praising
ZANU, at the same time being beaten with sticks. These
gatherings usually ended with public executions. Those
killed could be ex-ZIPRAs, ZAPU officials[6], or anybody
chosen at random, including women. Large numbers of
soldiers were involved in these events, sometimes as many
as two hundred, and often forty or more.

It is clear 5 Brigade was following orders when it
targeted civilians in this way, because the pattern is
similar throughout the regions affected.

In spite of the curfew, news spread and by early February the first efforts were being made to tell everyone what was happening and to get the Government to stop 5 Brigade activities. These efforts were met with denial on the part of Government officials. Minister Sekeramayi claimed the foreign press was "spreading malicious stories about the so-called atrocities." In March, officials from CCJPZ met with Prime Minister Mugabe, showing him evidence of atrocities. Mugabe made a public statement a few weeks later, on 6 April, denying the atrocities and accusing his critics of being "a band of Jeremiahs". However, a few days later, the curfew was lifted and it was agreed atrocities would be looked into.

The Government continued to make contradictory statements during these months, sometimes seeming to express regret at atrocities, and at other times clearly seeming to encourage them. The Minister of State Security, Emmerson Mnangagwa, told a Victoria Falls rally in March 1983 that the Government could choose to burn down "all the villages infested with dissidents." He added that, "the campaign against dissidents can only succeed if the infrastructure that nurtures them is destroyed."

In January 1984, 5 Brigade was deployed in Matabeleland South. Once more this coincided with a strict curfew. However, this time the curfew was very strictly applied to food supplies, in addition to restrictions on transport and movement around the region. It was the third successive year of drought and people had no food apart from drought relief from donors and what they could buy in stores. All drought relief food was stopped and all stores were closed.

5 Brigade used a more sophisticated strategy to intimidate the civilian population in 1984. In addition

*to the food curfew, thousands of civilians were detained
and transported to large detention centres where they
were then tortured. This meant that beatings and
killings in the village setting were less common than
before. In these big camps people did not know each
other, which makes it hard to work out how many
people were affected at this stage. At Bhalagwe camp in
Matobo District several thousand civilians were detained
at any one time and there were daily deaths in this
camp. The dead were thrown down Antelope Mine and,
in 1992, bones were taken out of the mine shaft. People
in the region claim there are many other mines with
bones in them.*

Villagers were made to dig their own graves and climb into them, where they were shot and, in some cases, buried while still moving. Villagers were made to dance on the graves of fellow villagers singing ZANU praise songs in Shona. In one documented case, villagers near Pumula Mission were not allowed to bury twelve of their people who had been murdered. Their bodies lay out in the open for all to see for a whole year.

In another documented case, two young girls who had been raped and made pregnant by army personnel the previous year, were shot and then bayoneted open to reveal the moving foetuses to other members of their community.

Women were stripped and beaten. In a number of recorded cases women had sharpened sticks forced into their vaginas. Men had their genitals tied in rubber and beaten.

The terrorization of the people of Matabeleland was widespread, systematic, and professionally executed over a lengthy period of time. The torture and murder of innocent people was calculated and supremely evil. The church, and everyone else, was largely silent through that time.

Eventually, Mengistu who "drained the sea" in Ethiopia had to flee. He came to Zimbabwe as an exile and is credited in some circles with having masterminded "Operation Murambatsvina" ("clearing up the rubbish"). In the period after the 2005 election it was decided that the shantytowns, which had grown up around the towns and were a hotbed for opposition support, should be demolished with State bulldozers.

In the Executive Summary of a United Nations report,[7] written at the behest of the Secretary General, Kofi Annan, the first paragraph reads:

On May 19, 2005, with little or no warning, the Government of Zimbabwe embarked on an operation to "clean-up" its cities. It was a "crash" operation known as "Operation Murambatsvina", referred to in this report as Operation Restore Order. It started in the Zimbabwe capital, Harare, and rapidly evolved into a nationwide demolition and eviction campaign carried out by the police and the army. Popularly referred to as "Operation Tsunami" because of its speed and ferocity, it resulted in the destruction of homes, business premises and vending sites. It is estimated that some 700,000 people in cities across the country have either lost their homes, their source of livelihood or both. Indirectly, a further 2.4 million people have been affected in varying degrees. Hundreds of thousands of women, men and children were made homeless, without access to food, water and sanitation, or healthcare. Education for thousands of school age children has been disrupted. Many of the sick, including those with HIV and AIDS, no longer have access to care. The vast majority of those directly and indirectly affected are the poor and disadvantaged segments of the population. They are, today, deeper in poverty, deprivation and destitution, and have been rendered more vulnerable.

It was indeed a shocking time. We were going through our own Operation Murambatsvina on the farms, but that wasn't an excuse for me to do nothing about it. I saw the bulldozers. I saw people being made to destroy their own houses. I drove past areas where there had been houses, but which now had been reduced to rubble, as though ravaged by war and not their own government. Next to the remains of their homes I saw occasional melancholy figures, wandering and bent looking, helpless and forlorn. Here and there were gaggles of cloaked figures by smoky fires, surrounded by a motley collection of belongings. It somehow seemed unreal. It took place so quickly. We were all caught by surprise.

2

WHAT DOES GOD CALL US TO DO?

CHRISTIANS AND THEIR RESISTANCE OR NON-RESISTANCE TO INJUSTICE IN ZIMBABWE AND THE WORLD

What does the Lord require of you but to do justice, to love mercy, and to walk humbly with your God. (Micah 6:8)

The concept of human rights and dignity has its origins in the biblical principle of the sanctity of human life – the Judeo-Christian belief that we are created individually in God's image and loved individually by an all-powerful, all-loving God. According to the secular French philosopher Jacques Derrida:

> *Today the cornerstone of international law is the sacred, what is sacred in humanity. You should not kill. You should not be responsible for a crime against the sacredness of man as your neighbour… In that sense, the concept of a crime against humanity is a Christian concept and I think there would be no such thing in the law today without the Christian heritage, the Abrahamic heritage and the biblical heritage.[1]*

Atheists and humanists acknowledge the importance of human rights and sanctity of life, but that belief is spiritual in origin.

The Bible is very clear on issues of injustice and the abuse of power. Isaiah stated, "Stop doing wrong, learn to do right! Seek justice, encourage the oppressed. Defend the cause of the fatherless, plead the case of the widow" (Isaiah 1:17). Later he chided, "Is not this the kind of fasting I have chosen: to loose the chains of injustice and untie the cords of the yoke, to set the oppressed free and break every yoke?" (Isaiah 58:6).

When injustice occurs, what is our response? My response to the injustice in Zimbabwe was much the same as many others, especially when it came to a government programme like Operation Murambatsvina with its systematic destruction of hundreds of thousands of people's homes and businesses – utter shock. Everyone was stunned because the devastation had taken place so quickly. We were caught off guard; this injustice was so blatant. Such a scenario had never entered anyone's minds, so consequently no one had given a thought to how they might respond. Such is the way with "blitzkrieg injustice"; it goes so far beyond "normal" that we stand rooted in shock, unable to process what is happening, let alone formulate an appropriate response. Injustice of any kind is like death: however expected it is, it still catches us by surprise.

Returning to our boxing metaphor: the most natural reaction of any person in the ring is to try to escape, to wriggle free from the violence. But how should those outside the ring, the onlookers, respond? Should they rush into the ring, risking themselves in being exposed to the same violence? Or should they just look on and not get involved. In the case of the policy of Operation Murambatsvina, sadly the church did not stand in front of the bulldozers that decimated people's homes. Few churches issued strong statements to the world's media.

Once the atrocities began, many churches in Bulawayo did open their doors and try to assist the homeless; and there was a more general awakening to the horrors of the injustice. Yet the church was lax in its response to block it. We were genuinely taken by surprise. Normally, governments do not suddenly, wilfully destroy multiple thousands of their citizen's homes. That is why blitzkrieg injustice works – it is impossible to expect the unexpected.

A further response to injustice may be that, over time, one becomes accustomed to repeated infringements. When patterns of injustice continue for many years, people tend to focus more on their personal survival than on sorting out the situation itself. Fear for personal safety becomes paramount. A conditioning process takes place so that people start to believe the lie that any action they take in response will be inadequate and of no consequence in stopping the oppression. When everything appears to be stacked against us, so often we decide to do nothing. It seems easy for evil to prevail when evil is allowed to play by unfair rules. The trouble with being on the side of good is that we have to play using rules that are fair!

I went to a rugby festival where my ten-year-old son, Stephen, was playing. He belongs to a very small, rural boarding school and his team were doing fantastically against the bigger schools. They were winning matches and playing excellent, clean rugby. At the end of the festival, however, in the last game they came up against a school much bigger than theirs – with much bigger children. Unfortunately there was a mix up and the referee didn't show up to officiate the game. Instead, the opposing team's coach volunteered to referee. Stephen's team, despite being smaller, did very well and they were ahead at half time. But as the second half progressed it became more and more apparent that the referee had developed "selective vision" and was no longer unbiased. He allowed his team to commit offences without being penalized, enabling them to score. Towards the end it became so blatant that everyone, even the other teams' parents on the sideline, were shaking their heads.

Of course, the inevitable happened and the team of bigger kids was able to run in just enough tries to win the game and walk off the pitch as the "winners". Afterwards, some of Stephen's team were so dispirited at the blatant dishonesty that they were crying. It was the injustice that upset them, not losing. They had prepared themselves for this tournament; they were tackling the big guys and hanging onto them like terriers, getting possession of the ball; they had given it their all and by rights they should have won. But they were destroyed by something that no one had prepared for – a referee who was applying the rules selectively and dishonestly.

I tried to comfort them. "Life isn't fair," I said, "but even if the rules get broken by the opposition, it is no license to break the rules ourselves. Even if the opposition win on paper, they will be the losers in the end if they don't play by the rules. If we play honestly and by the right rules and stand for those rules and do our best, never giving up, we will eventually be the winners." It seemed a little empty.

The conundrum that the church faces in times of blitzkrieg injustice is not a new one. Throughout church history there have been frequent times of trial, where governments have persecuted believers in unjust ways. The most challenging incidents in recent history were the injustices that occurred throughout Christian Europe in the 1930s and 1940s.

National Socialism, through Adolph Hitler and the Nazi party, was sweeping across Europe. Established Christian norms and laws were wilfully broken and those who were breaking the rules were winning. The Nazi creed was anti-Christian and deeply dangerous. But was anyone prepared to stand in the way of this gigantic, terrifying force moving in an avalanche of destruction? Martin Niemöller spoke out boldly and prophetically in a sermon in Berlin in 1934, the year after Hitler came to power:

> *We've been thrown into the Tempter's sieve, and he is shaking and the wind is blowing, and it must now become manifest whether we are wheat or chaff! Verily, a time of sifting has come upon us, and even the most indolent and peaceful person among us must see that the calm of meditative Christianity is at an end… it is testing time, and God is giving Satan a free hand, so he may shake us up and so that it may be seen what*

manner of men we are!… and he who is not ready to
suffer, he who called himself a Christian only because he
thereby hoped to gain something good for his race and his
nation is blown away like chaff by the wind of this time.[2]

There are numerous stories regarding Christians and the church losing their way in Nazi Europe amid government-sponsored blitzkrieg injustice. We need to learn from these. The persecution of the Jews was not something new. They had long been persecuted, even by the church. I was horrified to read what Martin Luther wrote in a booklet published in 1548 entitled "The Jews and Their Lies". Undeniably Luther played a vital role in breaking a yoke of oppression through the Reformation, bringing Christians back to a living faith. He was a brave and tireless champion for this cause. Yet, he lost his way when he wrote about the Jews:

What shall we as Christians do with this damned,
rejected race of the Jews? Since they live among us, and
we know about their lying and blasphemy and cursing,
we can not tolerate them if we do not wish to share their
lies, curses and blasphemy… we must prayerfully and
reverentially practice merciful severity.

What Luther meant by "merciful severity' was his proposal to set fire to Jewish synagogues and schools and to deprive Jews of their homes. He went so far as to say, "We are at fault in not slaying them… they must be driven from our country… we must drive them out like mad dogs."

Nearly 400 years later in November 1938, during Kristallnacht, when the synagogues were burnt and Jewish shops were looted throughout Germany, signalling what most historians consider to be the real start of the Holocaust, there was no public criticism from the churches. A full month later the Confessing Church asked its congregants, "To concern themselves with the material and spiritual distress of our Christian brothers and sisters of the Jewish race..."[3] but there was no public call for Christians to concern themselves with Jews who were not Christians.

Earlier that year, one week after the Austrians welcomed Hitler and the Reich into Austria in March 1938, the Austrian bishops met to bless Nazism, saying, "From inner conviction and with free will we, the undersigned Bishops of the Austrian church province, acknowledge joyfully that the national socialist movement... has committed greatly to the social politic for the German Reich..."[4]

The Slovakian bishops were no exception. Slovakia had become an independent State under the leadership of a priest. This church leader, Reverend Jozef Tiso, had another sixteen members of parliament under his presidency who were also priests – a full quarter of the members of the house. On 28 July 1940, Tiso met with Hitler in Salzburg and resolved to establish a more systematic policy of anti-Semitism in Slovakia. By September 1941 the Jewish Codex was drawn up, in which draconian anti-Jewish laws were promulgated. They set the scene to allow Slovakia to become the first country outside the Reich to deport Jews to extermination camps. Tiso was so keen to get rid of the Jews that he paid the German SS 500 Deutschmarks for every Jew who was deported, with the promise that they would "never return". On 26 March 1942, the first train load of 999 young women chugged out of the station on its way to Auschwitz. Over the next three months, 52,000 Jews had been deported, almost all to their deaths.

Fortunately, eventually, other church leaders in Slovakia did protest further deportations in a pastoral letter on 21 March 1943. This was read out in most of the churches, but there were only 20,000 Jews left in the country by then.

Thereafter, deportations were stopped until early 1945 when the Vatican, to its credit, did try to intervene when deportations were about to resume. Tiso wrote back to Pope Pius XII saying:

*The rumours about cruelties are but an exaggeration
of hostile enemy propaganda... the deportations were
undertaken in order to defend the enemy from his foe...
we owe this as [an expression] of gratitude and loyalty
to the Germans for our national sovereignty.*[5]

After the war Tiso was found guilty of crimes against humanity and hanged in his clerical robes on 18 April 1947.

Shortly after the first death train from Slovakia left, the first Jewish deportations to the death camps took place in France, Holland, and Belgium. According to Saul Friedländer, the assembly of cardinals and bishops in France welcomed the severe limitations imposed on French Jews. No member of the Catholic hierarchy expressed any protest regarding the racial statutes of October 1940 and June 1941, which enabled the Jews to be persecuted in the lead-up to their extermination. In the neighbouring country of Belgium, the Archbishop of Mechelen remained equally silent about the anti-Jewish edicts of 1940 and 1941.

In Poland, where the largest number of Jews in Europe lived, the church conveyed a message to the Polish government in exile in London on 15 July 1941: "The need to solve the Jewish question is urgent. Nowhere else in the world has that question reached such a climax, because no fewer than four million of these highly noxious and by all standards dangerous elements live in Poland."[6]

Bishop Konrad von Preysing of Berlin made a plea from the wilderness in January 1941. He wrote to the Pope:

*Your Holiness is certainly informed about the situation
of the Jews in Germany and in the neighbouring
countries. I would like to mention that I have been
asked by Catholics as well as by Protestants whether the
Holy See couldn't do something about this matter, issue
an appeal in favour of these unfortunate people.*[7]

Although the Pope replied, praising Bishop Preysing's sermon against euthanasia, he said not a word in relation to the persecution of the Jews.

In August 1941 the Vichy French enquired of the Vatican what the official church response was to anti-Jewish legislation. The French diplomat to the Holy See replied that, "although there existed a fundamental conflict between racial theories and Church doctrine, it did not follow that the Church necessarily repudiated every measure taken by particular countries against the Jews."[8]

And yet, Proverbs 24:11–12 entreats us to:

> *Rescue those being led away to death; hold back those staggering towards slaughter. If you say, "but we knew nothing about this" does not he who weighs the heart perceive it? Does not he who guards your life know it? Will he not repay each person according to what he has done?*

One excuse the church put forward to explain why it was so deficient in condemning the slaughter and not doing more to rescue victims was because, "it did not know what was going on". Hans-Rüdiger Minow, a spokesman for the Train of Commemoration, explained to the *Jerusalem Post* that 200,000 railway employees would have been involved in the deportations in the cattle trucks of the Sonderzug (special trains), where conditions were appalling and no food or water was given. The SS officer Kurt Gerstein recorded in his diary that on one train of 6,700 Jews, 1,450 were dead on arrival. In one transport from Corfu, which took eighteen days, the whole trainload of Jews was already dead by the time the train arrived. Those 200,000 employees knew what was going on, as would have others, but they were caught in the system and they carried on mechanically, transporting people to their deaths.

According to Friedlander, the only instance where a senior churchman publicly condemned the crimes being committed by the Third Reich was on 3 August 1941. Bishop Clemens von Galen preached a sermon at Munster Cathedral endorsing the pastoral letter of the previous month, which condemned the taking of innocent lives in the euthanasia programme. He preached on Luke 19:41: "As [Jesus] approached Jerusalem and saw the city, he wept over it." Jesus was weeping over the suffering he saw coming, when Jerusalem would be destroyed and the Jews would be persecuted. "Tears for misrule, the injustice and man's wilful refusal of Him and the resulting evils... It is a fearful thing when man sets his will against the will of God, and it is because of this that our Lord is lamenting over Jerusalem," Bishop Clemens said. He went on,

> *there are sacred obligations of conscience from which*
> *no one can release us and which we must fulfil, even*
> *at the price of death itself. At no time and under no*
> *circumstances whatsoever may a man, except in war and*
> *in lawful defence, take the life of an innocent person.*[9]

Bishop Clemens then explicitly described the innocent lives that were being taken in the euthanasia programme before cataloguing how each of the Ten Commandments was being wilfully disobeyed by the German Government. The sermon was reproduced all over Germany. The Nazi government immediately stopped the euthanasia programme – at least in a visible way. There was no other occasion in the history of the evils of Nazi rule where a prominent churchman voiced publicly the sins of the government.

We in the church cannot be naïve to the depravity of the human mind and the extent to which evil can master it. The deception of Satan is able to infiltrate right into the heart of the church and we must be, in Jesus' words, "as wise as serpents" when we discern what injustices are occurring around us.

Hitler knew of the potential problem of Christians speaking out and the church uniting to frustrate his evil designs. He took measures to destroy their independence early on. He made it illegal to give to charities, while churchmen were able to be controlled through the Church Tax, which the Reich could withhold from them if they did not toe the Nazi line. According to Hermann Rauschning, Hitler said to him in April 1933:

> *Neither Catholic nor Protestant has any future left; at least not for the Germans. Nothing will stop me stamping out Christianity in Germany, root and branch. One is either a Christian or a German. You cannot be both… the clergy will be made to dig their own graves. They will betray their God to us… they will betray anything for the sake of their miserable little jobs and income…[10]*

Although Rauschning's claims of what Hitler said to him have been discredited by some, the views expressed proved to be prophetic regarding the official church response to the widespread horrors of the German Government's crimes against humanity.

In Zimbabwe, the church has not been vocal either in condemning the injustices committed by the authorities. Although Zimbabwe boasts of being a Christian nation with churches everywhere – most of them full – the church has not generally concerned itself with justice issues at all. Church leaders do not preach sermons on what a Christian's response should be to injustice. Prayer marches are no longer held. The press is hardly ever issued with statements by church leaders about widespread, blatant government injustice.

Though we are in the world, Jesus tells us that "My kingdom is not of the world" (John 18:36). The trouble is, we often become so much part of the world that when its very fabric is torn asunder, we become disorientated and lost. Alternatively, we live in a holy huddle in the "other world", in a state of cocooned denial.

In a church in Bulawayo some time ago, where the film *Mugabe and the White African* was being shown, we had a discussion afterwards and Dr Peter Mundy, a world-renowned ornithologist, spoke up: "The trouble with you Christians," he said "is that you pray and you sing, but you do not act."

I received this as a challenge to all of us who call ourselves Christians.

In Paul's letter to the Ephesians he writes of our battle being against the "rulers, the authorities, the powers of this dark world and the spiritual forces of evil in the heavenly realms" (Ephesians 6:12). In this battle we need to oppose evil without either creating new evils, thereby becoming evil ourselves, or becoming impotent and irrelevant as Dr Mundy believed we are. Paul reveals that evil is something much bigger than its physical manifestation. Demonic forces are seldom mentioned in the Old Testament, but with the advent of Jesus, demons come up extensively. Demonic influence leads to the perversion of God's law, perverting the way in which governments are supposed to govern. Through them, corporate sin becomes established in nations.

Injustice stems from greed, selfishness, and pride and a brutal, demonic urge to dominate and control others at all costs. Manifestations of this include violent oppression, lawlessness, corruption, nationalism, and racism. The church needs to directly confront the crushing structural sins that are spiritual and demonic in origin within nations.

Ezekiel cries by the rivers of Babylon and expresses the heart of God regarding corrupt authorities:

> There is a conspiracy of her princes within her like a
> roaring lion tearing their prey; they devour people, take
> treasures and precious things and make many widows
> within her. Her priests do violence to my law… her
> officials within her are like wolves tearing their prey…
> for unjust gain… They mistreat the alien, denying them
> justice… I looked for a man among them who would
> build up the wall and stand before me in the gap on

behalf of the land so I would not have to destroy it…
(Ezekiel 22:25–30)

But Ezekiel's man who would "stand in the gap" wasn't to be found, so God destroyed the Promised Land: the Temple, the wall around Jerusalem, the vineyards, the flocks and the herds, the people and their homes. God is a God of justice. In the Psalms we read, "Righteousness and justice will be the foundation of your throne" (Psalm 89:14).

Unjust acts always seem to involve taking: taking life, taking liberty, taking dignity, taking property, taking the fruits of our love. When governments start taking rather than protecting, we as Christians have an obligation to stand up.

After being abducted and tortured I was in hospital in 2008. There were many other people there too, some in a much worse state than we were. Laura visited a man who had had his hands tied behind his back with barbed wire. His hands were then shattered by people hurling rocks down onto them. His kneecaps had been similarly smashed. Six weeks after this brutality he didn't even know if his family was alive or dead. At that time he was just one of tens of thousands of examples of the severe abuse of power by the authorities.

There are signs of hope in Zimbabwe though. Amid the chaos and suffering endured by Zimbabweans there is a huge move towards God. Crowds are flocking to church as never before. I spoke to a friend whom I'd not seen for some time. He is in the construction industry and had previously been kept busy putting up steel sheds for farmers. "You must be really struggling for work now," I commented.

"I've never been busier," he replied.

"You're pulling my leg!" I exclaimed.

"No," he said, "all these churches need new buildings. I am building one at the moment to seat twenty thousand people."

Within the church, however, there are people trying to control, manipulate, and negate the message regarding justice. They are attempting to achieve political control by infiltrating the church and professing to be Christian. At Easter 2012, the biggest stadium in the nation was not big enough to hold all the Christians for an Easter service. But the Minister of Information, Webster Shamu, tried to join the band that was leading worship and took the microphone.

Other infiltrators are also evident: Emmerson Mnangagwa, the feared former minister credited with masterminding much of the policy of "Gukurahundi" ("early rain that blows away the chaff") from his position as Minister of State Security declared himself to be a born-again Christian during the 2005 election. He said that he was like Saul, who changed his name to Paul. In 2010, as Minister of Defence, this *ngwenya,* or crocodile, as Mnangagwa is nicknamed, publicly declared at his brother's funeral: "For those of us comrades who were taught to destroy and kill and have seen the light in the last days of our lives, and will die in Christ, our rewards are in heaven."[11]

Another is Augustine Chihuri, the Commissioner of Police who allowed the farm seizures to proceed, along with all their violence, "Operation Murambatsvina"[12] ("clearing up the rubbish"), and the election violence using the selective application of the law. He too has declared that he is a born-again Christian. President Mugabe goes to mass and has dressed himself up in the white robes of the "Vapositori" sect, like the infamous former cabinet minister, Border Gezi. Before he died, Gezi started the notorious youth militia camps that the "green bombers" sprang from.

The Reserve Bank Governor, Gideon Gono, who brought the country to its knees by printing money and causing the most debilitating hyper-inflation in economic history (with hundred trillion dollar notes becoming worthless in days), laces his statements with biblical quotes.

Prime Minister Morgan Tsvangirai has been to Nigeria to see the "prophet" T. B. Joshua and has also taken to using the word of God, but some people struggle to see how sincerely.

The church is seen as an important constituency, so it is being infiltrated and used in what Zimbabwe has become well known for: the political agenda of covetousness, theft, and racism.

Within the Anglican Church a very effective political campaign took place to put a ZANU-PF politician in position. According to Revd Tim Neill, who stood against him, Bishop Kunonga had spent the previous fourteen years as a lecturer in political science at Chicago University in the USA. There he had fathered children by a woman who was not his wife. Early on in Bishop Kunonga's new post in the church, he took over the Hales farm in Nyabira. The Hales were unable to get their farm equipment off the land, so it was stolen from them – even though the bishop never used it to produce crops. Then in September 2004, about forty farm worker families were forced off the farm by police and their houses were burnt.

"Bishop" Kunonga said in May 2012:

> Whites like other aliens should not be allowed to own land and other properties in the country as they are strangers… I took 3,800 church properties in the region since their title deeds were in my name. There was no way the properties could remain under charge of the church controlled by whites and their black puppets. Bishops such as Julius Makoni, Chad Gandiwa and others are MDC-T and only want western interests furthered… those who participate in the land grab and future seizure of mines and other properties in the hands of aliens, will definitely enter the kingdom of God… The Prime Minister is good for nothing… Elections will give Zimbabweans the opportunity to choose between good (Mugabe) and death (Tsvangirai). Vote wisely. I am

a professor in my own right and would rate Mugabe's governance as "very good".[13]

Isaiah warns, "Woe to those who call evil good" (Isaiah 5:20). The wider Zimbabwe church remained silent in the face of this blasphemy.

The "career defining" visit to Zimbabwe in October 2011 by the Archbishop of Canterbury, Rowan Williams, had much to do with Kunonga appearing to outlive his usefulness to President Mugabe at the time. To his credit, the Archbishop did not legitimise what was wrong; instead he handed over a dossier to President Mugabe and spoke out against the injustices taking place against the Anglicans. After the heavily rigged elections of 31 July 2013 which saw Mugabe returned to power, the defrocked bishop and his cronies were reported to again be attempting to seize churches, orphanages and missions associated with the Church of England.

Through the history of the Bible we see justice and injustice rising and falling like waves on the sea. As the administration of justice collapses and the abuse of power becomes prevalent, terrible things happen to the nation of Israel. As the administration of justice rises with the turning to God, we see the right exercise of power, and God's blessings are poured out. Through the Bible, God's hatred of injustice is only rivalled by his hatred of idolatry.

Administering justice is a command:

> *Administer justice every morning; rescue from the hand*
> *of his oppressor the one who has been robbed or my*
> *wrath will break out and burn like fire because of the*
> *evil you have done – burn with no one to quench it.*
> (Jeremiah 21:12)

We, the church, need to be actively rescuing people from the hand of the oppressor.

Jesus castigates his people: "Woe to you Pharisees… you neglect justice and the love of God. You should have practised the latter without leaving the former undone" (Luke 11:42).

The failure of the wider church to stand against Nazi injustice and evil was utterly tragic. The Nazis used the two tools of the unjust to great effect: lies and fear through brutality. In 2001, my sister-in-law brought Dr Ingrid Landman from Harare to a meeting we were organizing. Ingrid told us the story of a church on the railway line to Auschwitz. An old, weeping man originally told the story. Hearing it was a defining moment for me. I repeat it here:

> *I lived in Germany during the Nazi Holocaust. I considered myself a Christian. I attended church since I was a small boy. We had heard the stories of what was happening to the Jews, but like most people today in this country, we tried to distance ourselves from the reality of what was really taking place. What could anyone do to stop it? A railroad track ran behind our small church, and each Sunday morning we would hear the whistle from the distance and then the clacking of the wheels moving over the track. We became disturbed when one Sunday we noticed cries coming from the train as it passed by. We grimly realized that the train was carrying Jews. They were like cattle in those cars!*
>
> *Week after week that train whistle would blow. We would dread to hear the sound of those old wheels because we knew that the Jews would begin to cry to us as they passed our church. It was so terribly disturbing! We could do nothing to help these poor miserable people, yet their screams tormented us. We knew exactly at what time that whistle would blow, and we decided the only way to keep from being so disturbed by the cries was to start singing our hymns. By the time the train came rumbling past*

*the churchyard, we were singing at the top of our voices.
If some of the screams reached our ears, we'd just sing
a little louder until we could hear them no more. Years
passed and no one talks about it much any more, but I
still hear that train whistle in my sleep. I can still hear
them crying out for help. God forgive all of us who called
ourselves Christians, yet did nothing to intervene.*

Pastor Dietrich Bonhoeffer was a man who stood out in the church
in Nazi Germany. He declared:

*We have been silent witnesses of evil deeds; we have
been drenched by many storms; we have learnt the arts
of equivocation and pretence; experience has made us
suspicious of others and kept us from being truthful
and open; intolerable conflicts have worn us down and
even made us cynical. Are we still of any use? What we
shall need is not geniuses, or cynics, or misanthropes, or
clever tacticians, but plain, honest, and straightforward
men. Will our inward power of resistance be strong
enough, and our honesty with ourselves remorseless
enough, for us to find our way back to simplicity and
straightforwardness?*[14]

He was very direct when he said, "We are not simply trying to
bandage the wounds of victims beneath the wheels of injustice,
we are to drive a spoke into the wheel itself!"[15]

James wrote:

*Suppose a brother or sister is without clothes and
daily food. If one of you says to him: "Go, I wish you
well; keep warm and fed," but does nothing about his
physical needs, what good is it. In the same way faith, if
not accompanied by action, is dead.* (James 2:15–17)

Jesus calls us to action: to preach the gospel by responding to hunger with food, to nakedness with clothes, to imprisonment with visitation, to the sick with medicine, to the beaten with bandages, and to injustice with justice.

Bonhoeffer said, "When Christ calls a man he calls him to die."

"Cheap grace," he said "is the grace we bestow on ourselves. Cheap grace is the preaching of forgiveness without requiring repentance, baptism without church discipline, Communion without confession... Cheap grace is grace without discipleship, grace without the cross, grace without Jesus Christ, living and incarnate."[16]

We pray in the prayer that Jesus taught us, "Your kingdom come... on earth as it is in heaven", but what part are we playing to bring God's kingdom, ruled by his "sceptre of justice" when that sceptre is dashed to the ground? Two truths apply to everything that God wants to do on this earth:

1. He could accomplish everything through his own supernatural power.
2. He chooses instead to accomplish it through the obedience of his people, which means we are being called to action.

As the church community we are not here to merely accommodate ourselves to the prevailing culture of injustice and indifference. We must be involved in learning how to rescue the oppressed; how to set prisoners free; how to break the yoke of injustice and ensure perpetrators cannot continue in their ways. God intends the church to penetrate the world with salt and light and so to change it – stopping the bacterial decay. He calls us to disperse the darkness. He calls us to action.

There are many excuses for not speaking or acting against injustice, and if our faith is not big enough we will do what is expedient and walk into the trap of complacency. If that happens then that which Isaiah warns of happens:

*So justice is driven back, and righteousness stands at
a distance; truth has stumbled in the streets, honesty
cannot enter. Truth is nowhere to be found, and whoever
shuns evil becomes a prey. The Lord looked and was
displeased that there was no justice. He saw that there
was no one, he was appalled that there was no one to
intervene.* (Isaiah 59:14–16)

When God's people did not stand for truth and justice, God stopped listening to their prayers. He didn't hear them, so their prayers could not be answered. We can't wait for God. God is waiting for us.

Shortly after witnessing the atrocities of injustice in Rwanda in 1994, where nearly a million people were hacked to death with machetes in a hundred days, Gary Haugen wrote:

*Evil and injustice thrive on moral ambiguity,
equivocation, confusion and the failure to commit.
Remembering that injustice is about power, and the
abuse of it, we must be aware that injustice is powerful,
strong and committed and in every case it will prevail
when we are uncertain, unsure and uncommitted.*[17]

The psalmist asks the question, "Who will rise up for me against the wicked; who will take a stand for me against evil doers?" (Psalm 94:16). We are commanded to, "Defend the cause of the weak and fatherless; maintain the rights of the poor and oppressed. Rescue the weak and the needy; deliver them from the hand of the wicked" (Psalm 82:3–4).

God calls us to action. There are four main reasons why the church often does not act in times of severe injustice:

1. The first and most overriding reason why Christians and others do not act against injustice is the Goliath of fear. In Zimbabwe

fear broods like a vast malevolent spirit over, around, and within the people. Fear paralyses. Fear warps our actions. Fear has us say, "If I get involved, what will happen to me or my family or my business?"

2. The second reason is because the truth does not course through us powerfully enough, and we allow ourselves to believe a theological lie. We deem action against injustice to be "political" and we say "the church mustn't get involved in politics". Some of us deceive ourselves that Zimbabwe is in a Nebuchadnezzar moment of chastisement, and we must somehow just take the evil submissively and not disturb it. Because whether it is Hitler, Stalin, Mao, Idi Amin, Mugabe, or the anti-Christ himself, we must "submit" meekly to the authorities.

3. The third reason is because we are discouraged. "How can I, little me, make a difference? I do not have any resources and the problem is so big!" Others say, "This is Africa, where so much injustice takes place and the rule of law is so little known!" Eventually that terrible thing called cynicism creeps into our hearts. C. S. Lewis said, "Despair is a greater sin than the sins that provoke it."[18] In God's kingdom there is no room for despair. Our hearts must always have hope that we can make a difference because we serve the God of all hope – the God who can break every chain.

4. The fourth reason is that we have become complacent and callous and are too busy. We feel we do not have time. I am sure the lawyer and the priest in the story of the Good Samaritan both had important business to attend to when they passed the beaten-up man on the road. There was a lack of conviction in their hearts that they were commanded by God to drop everything and act. I remember in 2008 hearing that the bodies of two activists, who had been shot dead, were lying on the side of the road. The people who saw them did nothing about those bodies. "This is Zimbabwe," they said to me.

The great evangelical theologian Carl Henry wrote of the evangelicals of the eighteenth and nineteenth centuries that when the Great Awakening happened,

> *their evangelical movement was spiritually and morally vital because it strove for justice and also invited humanity for regeneration, forgiveness and power for righteousness. If the Church preaches only divine forgiveness and does not affirm justice she implies that God treats immorality and sin lightly... we should be equally troubled that we lag in championing justice and fulfilling our evangelical mandate.*[19]

In Zimbabwe we live in a land similar to the land of the prophet Micah: "Both hands are skilled in doing evil; the ruler demands the gifts, the judge accepts the bribes, the powerful dictate what they desire – they all conspire together" (Micah 7:3).

But Micah doesn't accept the status quo. He gets active and fired up and says, "As for me I am filled with power, with the spirit of the Lord, and with justice and might, to declare to Jacob his transgression, to Israel his sin" (Micah 3:8).

This is what it is all about. The wicked say, "he won't call me to account" (Psalm 10:13), but we can! Jesus says, "you are the light of the world... let your light shine before men" (Matthew 5:14–16). We need to be the light exposing the darkness. We need to be Christians with the mission of alleviating suffering by upholding the truth. When we see injustice we need to ask, "Who is the victim? What is the injury? How can I help? How can I expose the perpetrators so that they do not do this to the next person? Who can help me?"

If the church is to truly take its place in nations where governments stumble, churches need to have groups involved in justice missions. Prayer groups need to be praying and asking for God's wisdom, not man's wisdom, to act for justice in our communities and our nations. Wisdom needs to be sought to understand the spirit behind the structural evil. Faith needs to be sought to trust that the power of God is more powerful than the power of evil. But if godly people fail to take responsibility, playing their part in transforming societies of injustice, the scourge of corruption and evil will continue to grow like a cancer in our land.

Martin Niemöller, the German theologian and former president of the World Council of Churches after World War II, said about his incarceration in Nazi Germany:

> *First they came for the socialists and I did not speak out because I was not a socialist. Then they came for the trade unionists, and I did not speak out because I was not a trade unionist. Then they came for the Jews, and I did not speak out because I was not a Jew. Then they came for me, and there was no one left to speak for me.*[20]

Jesus said, "The spirit of the Lord is upon me, because he has anointed me... to release the oppressed" (Luke 4:18).

Our prayer must be: "Here am I, Lord, send me."

Christians are here on earth to help set others free from physical, spiritual, and mental oppression. Until we pray, "Send me" and overcome fear, theological lies, discouragement, and complacency, the killing, stealing, and destruction will continue. In John 10 Jesus spoke about the "thief" coming to "kill, steal and destroy". Good, committed watchmen are required if the thief is to be prevented from carrying out his work in our hearts, our churches and our nations. As Isaiah wrote, "The work of justice shall be peace and the effect of justice, quietness and assurance forever" (Isaiah 32:17).

But if we do not work for justice, the whirlwind of destruction will continue to blow through the land – on and on and on.

3

HOW NATIONS BECOME POOR AND HUNGRY

THE EROSION OF PROPERTY RIGHTS AND THE RULE OF LAW

I have come to realize that people living in countries where justice and the rule of law are intact have little appreciation for how the law protects life, liberty, and property. Neither do they understand how foundational the proper function of law, especially regarding property rights, is in eradicating poverty. It is taken for granted, in places where property rights exist, that "what is mine is mine" and "what is yours is yours" – and that any infringement of this status quo without agreement is fundamentally wrong.

The existence of property rights creates a system of ownership that minimizes disputes and maximizes the protection and productive use of each person's property. Titled land and property rights have a long, tumultuous history in many lands, but especially in Zimbabwe. The issue came all the more to the fore from the millennium onwards in the light of a dramatic economic collapse. Land invasions were orchestrated to intimidate farmers and farm workers ahead of the 2000 election. Property rights were usurped in a fundamental and systematic way.

Ayn Rand, a Russian Jew, lived through the Russian Revolution in 1917, which saw the abolition of private property. As a teenage girl she saw her father's chemist shop seized. She managed to get to America as a young adult where she lived for the rest of her life. There she was able to see how property rights worked to feed and build America, and export food to the people of Russia from whence she had come. She wrote profoundly,

> *The right to life is the source of all rights – and the right to own property is their only implementation. Without right to property no other rights are possible. Since man has to sustain his life by his own effort, the man who has no right to the product of his effort has no means to sustain his life. The man who produces while others dispose of his product is a slave.[1]*

The word "property" comes from the same root as the word "proper". In other words, it is rooted in morality. Symond Fiske, a South African economist, points out that,

> *wherever communities are poor it is always because people and their governments have been trying to take a short cut to wealth and affluence. Instead of formulating and heeding [moral] codes that respect ownership, they harass, raid and discourage folk who do… In reality, the only difference between theft and redistributive taxation is the size of the gang.[2]*

It is no coincidence that the earliest documented transfer of property rights to land in the history of the world is recorded in the Bible. It was in Hebron in 1675 BC when Abraham purchased the Cave of the Patriarchs, with a field and trees, from Ephron the Hittite for 400 shekels (about 6 kg) of silver. The transaction is described in detail in Genesis 23:3–20.

There are three fundamental biblical principles relating to property rights:

1. The first is the prohibition of theft, enshrined in the eighth commandment in Exodus 20:15, "You shall not steal", by which a person's property is afforded protection. The commandments "You shall not covet your neighbour's house" and "You shall not covet your neighbour's wife, or his manservant or maidservant, his ox or donkey, or anything that belongs to your neighbour" (Exodus 20:17) are meaningless unless we first observe another's ownership of property and don't attempt to steal it. We are to be faithful stewards of that which God gives us, and we are to respect the rights of others to do the same. As Irving E. Howard says, "The commandment… is the clearest declaration of the right to private property in the Old Testament."[3]

   The controversial theologian, Rousas Rushdoony, goes further: "The attack on private ownership is also an attack on God because it despises His law."[4] God's law is holy and it is absolutely central to who God is. The first thing God gave to the children of Israel when they came out of slavery, an independent nation, was the law. Mount Sinai trembled violently and was covered in smoke and the sound of a trumpet became louder and louder. God himself inscribed the tablets of stone with his own finger. The Ark of the Covenant, which contained the tablets of stone on which the commandments were written, went ahead of the nation. It even went before the army as the first thing to cross into the Promised Land forty years later – and the River Jordan dried up before it.

   The amazing Temple of Solomon was built around the Ark of the Covenant in which the law was housed. It was by administering justice and righteousness through the law in truth, that Israel became the superpower of its day. It was because of the law, and our unfaithfulness to it, that Jesus had to come to die for us in fulfilment of the law. Following "laws" that contradict God's law has always resulted in certain disaster.

2. The second principle of property rights is that the world ultimately belongs to God (not to the State), as exemplified in

the Psalms: "The earth is the Lord's, and all it contains, the world and those who dwell in it" (Psalm 24:1). "The world is mine and all it contains" (Psalm 50:12). "The whole earth is mine" (Exodus 19:5). We must not think that we are the absolute owners of anything. What we have we must not hold with overly tight fists, because ultimately it belongs to God. What we have should be used to bless others.

3. The third principle of property rights is a corollary to the second: humans are temporary tenants upon God's property. As King David said, "For we are but sojourners before you, and tenants, as all our fathers were" (1 Chronicles 29:15). As such, we must try to leave what we are given in good order for those who are to come after us.

It is important to understand how property rights were involved in the foundation and birth of civilizations. God gives people possession of the earth to extend the boundaries of his kingdom as they fulfil their calling in obedience to the truth. The Ahab-type confiscation or theft of property (see 1 Kings 21) has always been an attack upon his kingdom and its advance.

When a man is secure in the possession of his property, he has an area of freedom and dominion that is beyond the reach of other men. If no man and no State can reach in to tax and confiscate his property, man can enjoy true freedom and great security whether he is prosperous or poor. Every attack on private property is, therefore, an attack on man's fundamental freedom.

Man's freedom and security in the possession of his property is not only basic to man's independence from dictatorship; a man has independence if he can act independently of other men and the State, and if he can make his stand in the confidence of freedom.

Rousas Rushdoony said, "Every attack on private property therefore is also an attack on the powers of free men as well as their liberty."[5]

In every dictatorial regime there is a tussle between godly law, expressed in the private ownership of property, and man's law in the form of State ownership. Karl Marx and Friedrich Engels declared in their 1848 Communist Manifesto that the right to hold individual private property was a crime against the State. Their first "commandment" called for the "abolition of property in land and application of all rents of land to public purposes". Their third commandment abolished "all right of inheritance".

Both of these edicts sought to overrule the biblical order of protecting against the theft of property and encouraging inheritance.

Laws like those in Zimbabwe allow a single entity – the State – to consolidate its power. From this position of consolidation the State's creeping control influences individuals and their families, the church, the education system, and every other institution God ordained for the proper running of society. The State, therefore, becomes sovereign and owner, displacing God as the absolute ruler.

Those who deny the individual's right to own property, ignoring the biblical mandate of stewardship, are flouting God's order for society. In biblical terms, the ownership of property is important in the context of a man fulfilling his and his family's calling under God. It ties a person to their past and has a role to play in their future. This is why Naboth, in 1 Kings, was unwilling to sell his vineyard: "The Lord forbid that I should give you [Ahab] the inheritance of my fathers" (1 Kings 21:3).

Calvin Beisner asks the pointed question, "Why does Scripture require restitution, including multiple restitution, in cases of theft, even if paying the restitution requires selling oneself into slavery?"[6] (see Exodus 22:3). Immediately after the Ten Commandments, two of which deal specifically with the protection of private property, the Scriptures devote fifteen verses to the detailed laws relating to private property. People who steal or cause damage to private property are subject to severe penalties.

Our right to own property stems from our God-given responsibility to be productive and to be good stewards. After

God thrust Adam and Eve out of the Garden of Eden, he decreed that they (and we) would face a lifetime of hard work (Genesis: 3:17–19). God mercifully allows our hard work to reward us with property. The very existence of private property encourages our diligence and fruitfulness: "Lazy hands make a man poor, but diligent hands bring wealth" (Proverbs 10:4).

When we understand private property in the context of godly stewardship, we better understand our need to work and serve others – rather than pursuing the selfish goal of accumulating more and more to consume ourselves. In this sense, property ownership encourages the wise use of scarce resources. The nationalization of property, such as has taken place in Zimbabwe under Marxist totalitarian ideology, provides no such incentive.

Udo Middelmann comments profoundly, "True communion and true community are based upon property rights – for unless a person owns something he can share, there can be no community."[7]

In the early civilizations in Samaria and Babylonia, from where Abraham had come, the right to hold land as private property was already in force. The king, the theoretical owner of all the land by "divine right", had long before distributed it among his vassals. Careful surveys were made and inscribed stones set up on the boundaries of a property, indicating the possessor and invoking the curse of the gods on any who should interfere with property rights.

As a result of this institutionalized protection of private property, sophisticated irrigation schemes were set up and an agricultural revolution took place that had far-reaching effects. At its height, over 4,000 years ago, the irrigation system put in place in the Sumerian civilization under strict laws of private ownership covered over 2.5 million hectares. Detailed laws protecting private property were written, administered, and enforced, and the people flourished. It is hard to visualize this advanced, extensive development over 4,000 years ago without electric pumps, combustion engines, hi-tech surveying equipment, advanced transport systems, telephones, or refrigeration. Two and a half million hectares is ten times the area that Zimbabwe could irrigate at the height of its agricultural development at the turn of the twenty-first century!

Studies of other great civilizations reveal that property rights were essential and central to the prosperity and success of them all. On the continent of Africa, private ownership of land in the civilization of ancient Egypt was well established in the days when Joseph was in charge of all the land under the Pharaoh. As early as the middle of the third millennium BC, a sense of ownership was well developed. Egyptian texts written 4,400 years ago in honour of a god known as Uha say,

> *I was a commoner of repute, who lived on his own*
> *property, ploughed with his own span of oxen, and sailed*
> *in his own ship, and not through that which I had*
> *found in the possession of my father, honoured Uha.[8]*

The Bible tells us that, "Joseph bought all the land in Egypt for Pharaoh. The Egyptians one and all sold their fields because the famine was so severe for them. The land became Pharaoh's... however he did not buy the land of the priests" (Genesis 47:20–26).

There was a specific legal system of ownership that was sacrosanct. Pharaoh bought the land and the people, before the days of food aid, were pleased to have something to sell so that they could get money to buy food.

The prosperous civilizations of the ancient Greeks, and the Romans after them, had property rights as part of the founding principles of their remarkable cultures. G. F. Rehmke writes,

> *The powers of the early polis (city states) were limited by*
> *the same Greek tradition that served to protect private*
> *property: a deep respect—even worship—of the family*
> *"... the men of the early ages... arrived... by virtue of*

*their belief, at the conception of the right of property;
this right from which all civilization springs, since
by it man improves the soil, and becomes improved
himself"... "The appropriation of land for public utility
was unknown among the ancients. Confiscation was
resorted to only in case of condemnation to exile."[9]*

Antigone by the Greek playwright Sophocles focuses on the existence of a higher law that included property rights that even the king could not ignore. Antigone, the tragic heroine, disobeys the direct orders of Creon, the king, and buries her brother according to the sacred rituals. She tells the king:

*Nor did I think your orders were so strong that you, a
mortal man, could over-run the gods' unwritten and
unfailing laws. Not now, nor yesterday's, they always
live, and no one knows their origin in time. So not
through fear of any man's proud spirit would I be likely
to neglect these laws...*

Solon, a successful merchant and accomplished poet, revised Athenian laws in 594 BC to grant fuller property rights to a wider range of Greeks, allowing smaller, non-aristocratic farmers to own property. This led to a remarkable blossoming of industry and intellectual progress. Victor Davis Hanson points out that the disciplined life and hard labour on the thousands of small, independent farms, "developed Greek character, generated Greek wealth and defended Greek city-states". Family-owned and operated farms provided both the wealth and the defence for early ancient Greek cities. Their achievement, argues Hanson, "was the precursor in the West of private ownership, free economic activity, constitutional government, social notions of equality, decisive battle and civilian control over every facet of the military".[10]

The sanctity of private property and contract, shared by most Greek city-states and by Rome, profoundly influenced the economic success upon which the agricultural and industrial revolutions were eventually founded, bringing economic prosperity and development in the Western civilizations.

Jeremiah describes in detail a title deed that he bought when he knew that the Israelite exile in Babylon was imminent, over 2,600 years ago. He takes scrupulous care to attest the deeds of purchase and then preserve them.

> *I bought the field at Anathoth from my cousin Hanamel and weighed out for him seventeen shekels of silver. I signed and sealed the deed and had it witnessed and weighed out the silver on the scales. I took the deed of purchase – the sealed copy containing the terms and conditions as well as the unsealed copy... the God of Israel says houses and vineyards will again be bought in this land.* (Jeremiah 32:9–15)

The passage continues with God saying:

> *As I have brought this great calamity on this people so I will give them all the prosperity I have promised them. Once more fields will be bought in this land of which you say, "it is a desolate waste without men or animals..."* (vv. 42–43)

A direct result of the abolition of property rights is that the land becomes a "desolate waste". Before, when property rights were sacrosanct within the law, Israel had become the most powerful nation on earth. God promises that as a result of the re-establishment of property rights, prosperity would ensue.

Two and a half thousand years later, Zimbabwe moved from being the "breadbasket of Africa" to a "desolate waste" for exactly the same reason. Prosperity was only re-established in Israel when God ordained the restoration of the right to own private property and land could be bought and sold again.

Jeremiah's act of purchasing land was an act of hope for the future of returning exiles, helping them realize that God had done what he promised he would do. He knew that in law, his title deeds would stand the test of time and form part of the godly foundation upon which God's chosen people would rebuild the Promised Land after the exile.

In the book of Ruth, written 3,000 years ago, a little before Israel was at the height of its power, we read how Ruth went to glean leftover grain and "found herself working in a field belonging to Boaz" (Ruth 2:3). Throughout that chapter there is a sense of the productivity of that land. All the people are working diligently and the fruitful activity is taking place within this privately owned area. In Chapter 4 we read how Boaz "bought from Naomi all the property of Elimelech, Kilion and Mahlon" (v. 9). Notice that Boaz "bought" this land. There was no communal system of patronage. Investment took place and was duly protected.

History shows that without private property, nations starve. That is why God gave the Israelites the land in demarcated, protected portions and promised curses on anyone who stole land from another. Deuteronomy 27:17 declares, "Cursed is the man who moves his neighbour's boundary stone." The Bible explains what the curse will be if we do not follow "all his commands" (28:15) (including the theft of property):

> *You will be cursed in the city and cursed in the country.*
> *Your basket and your kneading trough will be cursed.*
> *The fruit of your womb will be cursed and the crops of*
> *your land, and the calves of your herds and the lambs of*
> *your flocks.* (28:16–18)

We have seen this curse take effect before our eyes in Zimbabwe.

Conversely, Deuteronomy says that those who,

> *fully obey the Lord your God and carefully follow all*
> *his commands… you will be blessed in the city and*
> *blessed in the country. The fruit of your womb will be*
> *blessed and the crops of your land and the young of your*
> *livestock… your basket and your kneading trough will*
> *be blessed.* (28:1–5)

Isaiah prophesizes about the kingdom to come and highlights it as the blueprint for how society ought to be run under the guidance of godly leadership: "no longer will they build houses and others live in them, or plant and others eat… they will not toil in vain or bear children doomed to misfortune" (Isaiah 65:21–23).

Micah 2 contains a passage we have read often:

> *Woe to those who plan iniquity, to those who plot evil*
> *on their beds! At morning light they will carry it out*
> *because it is in their power to do it. They covet fields and*
> *seize them, and houses and take them. They defraud*
> *a man of his home, a fellowman of his inheritance.*
> (Micah 2:1–2)

Micah goes on to discuss the consequences of this theft: "Therefore, the Lord says: 'I am planning disaster against this people, from which you cannot save yourselves'" (v. 3).

In Micah 4 there is a passage of hope about the coming kingdom, showing how things are designed to be under the rule of law and peace, with security in the ownership of private property: "Every man will sit under his own vine and his own fig-tree, and no-one will make them afraid" (v. 4).

The New Testament is equally clear in its assumption of the existence of a system of private ownership of land and property. Jesus talks about people owning land in the parable of the rich farmer, who sadly failed to store up his treasures in heaven (Luke 12). In one parable Jesus talks about a "landowner" with a vineyard (Matthew 20:1). In another he tells the story of a different landowner who rented out his estate when he went on a journey. The lessees wanted to steal what he had, so they ended up killing the landowner's son in order to "take his inheritance". Jesus pointed out that the landowner would "bring those wretches to a wretched end". Private ownership of land is God-ordained for the ordering of society and the feeding of the people.

The apostle Paul's exhortation to "steal no longer" is a clear warning to anyone who takes private property or anything else away from another. Paul says to the Ephesians, "He who has been stealing must steal no longer but must work, doing something useful with his own hands..." (Ephesians 4:28).

The confiscation of property through theft (Exodus 20:15) or by governmental decree, as in the Ahab and Jezebel case described in the story of Naboth's vineyard (1 Kings 21), has been replicated in dictatorial regimes such as in Zimbabwe.

> *Then the word of the Lord came to Elijah the Tishbite: "Go down to meet Ahab king of Israel, who rules in Samaria. He is now in Naboth's vineyard, where he has gone to take possession of it. Say to him, 'this is what the Lord says: Have you not murdered a man and seized his property?' Then say to him, 'This is what the Lord says: In this place where dogs licked up Naboth's blood, dogs will lick up your blood – yes yours!'"* (1 Kings 21:18–19)

Elijah found the king on his stolen property and said, "I have found you... because you have sold yourself to do evil..." (1 Kings 21:20). God put a terrible judgment on the king, the queen, and their family because he considered them to have committed a terrible sin. Nowhere else in the Bible do we read of such a terrible curse being put on a ruler.

Sir Thomas More, when he had refused to recognize Henry VIII as head of the church, defended himself in his trial (immortalized in Robert Bolt's *A Man for all Seasons*), saying, "The maxim is 'Qui tacet consentire': the maxim of the law is: silence gives consent."

The Christian church in Zimbabwe and other totalitarian states has endorsed the "theft of Ahab" by its silence. Silence has done more to allow the horrors of modern history to continue than anything else.

Thousands of years of experiments with State ownership of the land have resulted in nothing but failure and tragedy – Fascism, Nazism, and Communism have all denied God's law. In the "Great Leap Forward" in China, over 30 million people died of starvation over a period of four years – the greatest famine in the history of the world. This was the result of Chairman Mao spurning God's laws on property rights. During the years of State ownership of land in Russia, the country was in constant need of feeding by the West. With the re-establishment of property rights in Russia, its wheat production grew from 31 million tons (5 per cent of world production) to 62 million tons (10 per cent of world production) in a single decade (1999–2009). In the USA, with only a third of the arable land of Africa, approximately 320 million tons of maize is produced annually (about 40 per cent of world production), while in the whole of Africa, we only manage to produce 60 million tons (about 7 per cent of world production).

Primarily because nearly all African governments in sub-Saharan Africa have traditionally denied their people proper land ownership and protection systems, Africa is producing less than 10 per cent of what it could be producing if property rights were properly established. In the same decade that Russia doubled its wheat production, wheat production in Zimbabwe fell by over 90 per cent (see Figure 2 on p. 73).

Jesus was able to tell us the most important proposition in the economics of property rights. Jesus was trying to make an important point, but his listeners weren't getting it, so he gave them a simple parable they would understand:

> *The good shepherd lays down his life for the sheep. The*
> *hired hand is not the shepherd who owns the sheep. So*
> *when he sees the wolf coming, he abandons the sheep and*
> *runs away. Then the wolf attacks the flock and scatters it.*
> *The man runs away because he is a hired hand and cares*
> *nothing for the sheep. I am the good shepherd; I know*
> *my sheep and my sheep know me.* (John 10:11–14)

Jesus knew all about shepherds. The first people that the angel told about the birth of Jesus were the shepherds. Jesus' forefather, David, was a shepherd boy from Bethlehem who killed the lions and bears that tried to take his sheep. David was not a hired hand. He was the owner's son and heir. Thus he risked his life for his father's sheep.

Jesus' point was: people will not care for a resource they do not own as well as they will care for a resource that they do. Any law that turns a blind eye to this simple, fundamental truth is destined for disaster.

When the New Testament was translated from Greek into English nearly 400 years ago, the translators were reportedly puzzled about how exactly to translate the word *hupostasis*. It seemed to be some kind of business terminology not found in classical Greek literature. All they could determine was that it meant something fairly substantial, so they translated it as "substance", such as, "Faith is the substance of things hoped for, the evidence of things not seen" (Hebrews 11:1 KJV).

Hundreds of years later, archaeologists uncovered the charred ruins of an old inn in northern Israel. There they found a small iron chest containing the valuable papers of some Roman noblewoman who had apparently been staying in the inn while visiting properties she owned in the area. Most of the papers in the chest had the word *hupostasis* written in large Greek letters across the top. They were the title deeds to her properties. They were the proof that she owned them.

I find this story fascinating. "Faith" is fundamental to our spiritual lives as Christians and synonymous here with a "title deed". A title deed is fundamental to our physical lives in the world and synonymous with our faith. We could therefore translate Hebrews 11:1, "Now faith is the title deed to things hoped for." If our faith were to be somehow taken away, it would leave us without hope of the life to come. Similarly, when property title deeds are confiscated, there is little hope of nations meeting their physical needs and developing.

At their height, property rights extended to a little less than 40 per cent of the total land area of Zimbabwe. The majority of the agricultural land has always been held in a communal system, vested in the president. The communal farmers have never been given title deeds or any kind of formal ownership of the land that they occupy. As a result they find it almost impossible to secure financial credit, since they own nothing of value to use as an asset to secure a loan to develop their land. Successful neighbours are unable to buy neighbouring farms to ensure economies of scale and competitive efficiency. What is more, the communal farmer is subject to the whims of the chief and the spiritual and political hierarchies in his district. He is not an independent person, able to run his life in an independent way. Even his planting dates have traditionally been dictated to him. The communal farmer is bound to a subsistence existence for evermore, unless the communal system can be broken. A spirit of inertia will sit over the land and its people until it is.

In the years following 1980 the Zimbabwean Government bought many farms from commercial farmers, totalling around 3.6 million hectares. The title to this land was immediately vested in the president, and the land became largely unproductive. Like the communal people, they were now dependent on the authorities and destined to eke out a life of subsistence dependence. I saw many barns being taken down so that the bricks could be sold and irrigation pipes being cut up to make pots. Irrigation systems fell into disrepair, and production and employment levels plummeted. Plantations died, and trees were chopped down so that firewood could be sold.

The next stage of retrogressive land reform saw the violent land invasions begin in 2000. These were designed first to reward the party faithful with farms and second to bring the people under control by taking away their property rights and forcing the large population of farm workers into a position of fear and dependence on the ruling party. From this point of view, the farm invasions were a resounding success. The critical farm worker swing voters were so intimidated that they did not *dare* vote for the opposition, and Mugabe won an election he would otherwise have lost. In order to capitalize on this success, the ruling party continued their

FIGURE 1

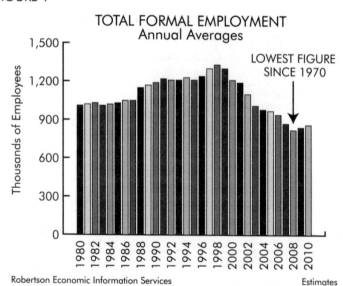

Robertson Economic Information Services

Estimates

invasions. When they managed to claw back a sizeable majority in Parliament in 2005, they were able to erode property rights further by allowing the State to seize farms simply by publishing a notice in a newspaper. All rights of owners to challenge such acquisitions in the courts were taken away.

The graphs below illustrate very clearly what happened when property rights were taken away in 2000. Figure 1 shows that, despite the population growing from 7 million in 1980 to 12 million people in 2010, formal employment was nearly 20 per cent less in 2010 than in 1980.

Wheat production (see Figure 2) is dependent on organized irrigation systems being developed and maintained. Without property rights it is difficult to do this. There was a severe drought in 1995. In the years since 2000 the majority of irrigation dams have remained full but much of the expensive infracture has been stolen or destroyed.

FIGURE 2

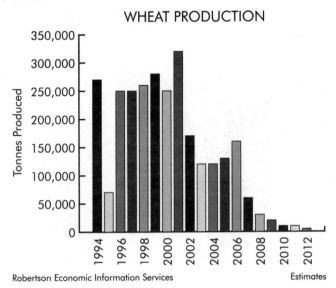

WHEAT PRODUCTION

Robertson Economic Information Services   Estimates

FIGURE 3

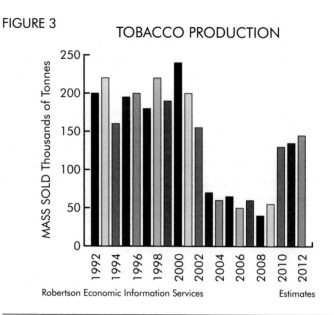

FIGURE 4

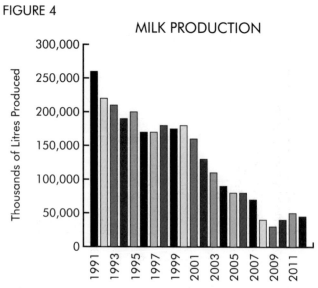

Without the destruction of property rights, it is estimated by the Zimbabwe Tobacco Association that tobacco production (Figure 3) would have been in excess of 500 million kilograms by now if the country's growth rate had followed a similar pattern to the other main tobacco exporter, Brazil, over the last decade. The trouble with the current, small-scale production is that it is dependent on firewood for the curing process, so large areas of indigenous bush are being cut to try to sustain it each year. Government figures estimate 300,000 hectares of indigenous forests in Zimbabwe are now cut down each year for curing tobacco. The consequences of deforestation on this scale will be extremely serious.

Milk production (Figure 4) relies on the stockfeed industry being in good order. Because Zimbabwe cannot even feed its own people, stockfeed has become scarce.

In the late 1970s beef production (Figure 5) was larger in financial terms than any other commodity, including tobacco.

FIGURE 5

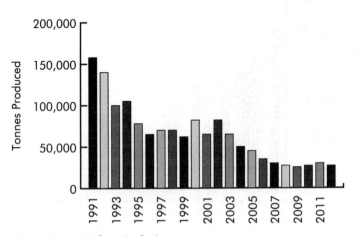

BEEF PRODUCTION

Robertson Economic Information Services

FIGURE 6

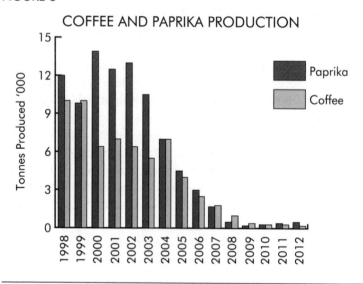

COFFEE AND PAPRIKA PRODUCTION

FIGURE 7

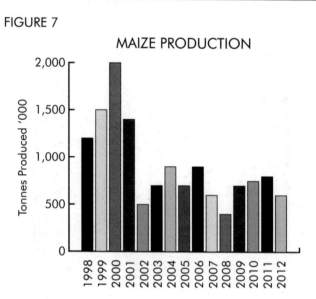

MAIZE PRODUCTION

With the government purchasing many of the big ranches for resettlement, uncontrolled veldt fires, and stock spreading disease through uncontrolled movement, the cattle industry has collapsed dramatically to less than a fifth of what it was.

All plantation crops such as coffee (see Figures 6) are long term. To recover coffee production needs long-term investment and great commitment. Without property rights, this confidence is not possible.

In no year since property rights were taken away has maize production (Figure 7) been enough even remotely to meet national demand. Food aid has been required every single year for more than a decade. Never had Zimbabwe or Rhodesia before it ever required food aid prior to the destruction of property

FIGURE 8

ZIMBABWE'S RAINFALL
Mean Annual Figures in Millimetres

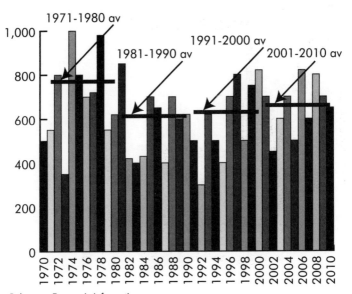

Robertson Economic Information

rights. Apologists of the land seizures often blame the problem on drought. This is a flawed argument (see Figure 8).

The manufacturing industry (Figure 9 and 10) in Zimbabwe has traditionally been very dependent on a healthy commercial agricultural sector. Going around some of the industrial areas today, particularly in Bulawayo, is like going around ghost towns.

The manufacturing sector in 2013 is only 60 per cent of its 1980 levels and is very much lower than in the late 1960s. Seventy per cent of raw materials came traditionally from the agricultural sector.

It has been reported that the dramatic drop in GDP (Figure 11) has outstripped all records around the world for peacetime economic decline.

Five billion dollars in 1980 had the buying power of approximately 10 billion dollars in 1997, when the Zimbabwean economy was at its height. As such, the GDP did not decline much

---

FIGURE 9

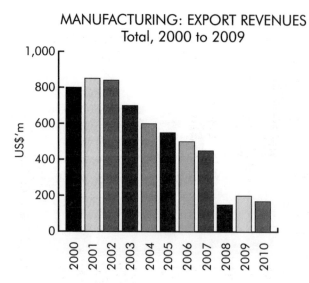

MANUFACTURING: EXPORT REVENUES
Total, 2000 to 2009

Robertson Economic Information Services

FIGURE 10

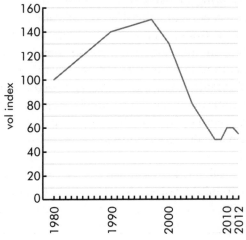

MANUFACTURING SECTOR
PERFORMANCE SINCE 1980

FIGURE 11

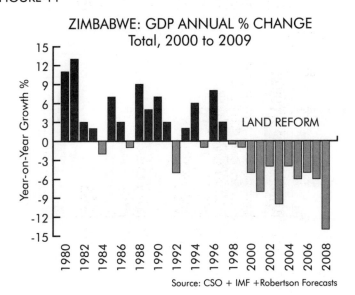

ZIMBABWE: GDP ANNUAL % CHANGE
Total, 2000 to 2009

LAND REFORM

Source: CSO + IMF +Robertson Forecasts

in real terms in the first two decades after independence. In the next decade, through the years of the destruction of property rights, GDP plummeted to a third of what the buying power was in 1980, despite the population having increased from 7 million to approximately 12 million.

The elite, of course, remain very rich. The cars, the mansions, and the glitz of the ruling clique are famous.

All the countries shown in Figure 12 had a significant positive growth rate from the year 2000 when Zimbabwe was the biggest of the six comparable economies listed. By 2009 only Malawi had a smaller economy.

Figure 13 shows a GDP per capita comparison between Botswana and Zimbabwe from 1980. It is worth noting that the Botswana GDP was 1.6 billion dollars in 1980 – only a little larger than the Zimbabwean economy at that time. By 2008 it was 26 billion dollars – over six times the size of the Zimbabwean economy (Figure 14).

FIGURE 12

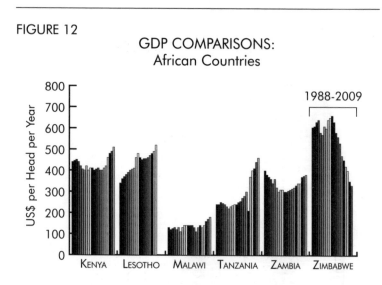

GDP COMPARISONS:
African Countries

Source: IMF Africa Dept & World Economic Outlook

FIGURE 13

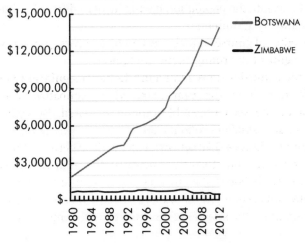

GDP PER CAPITA COMPARISON:
Zimbabwe and Botswana

FIGURE 14

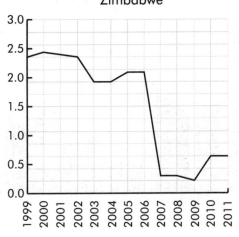

GDP PER CAPITA (US$):
Zimbabwe

Source: Index Mundi

In 2013 a new draft constitution was finalized in Zimbabwe to cement the property rights clauses that made food production and GDP plummet so devastatingly. The infamous Section 56 is a quintessentially Orwellian law regarding discrimination. It says almost exactly what was written in *Animal Farm* by George Orwell: "All animals are equal, but some animals are more equal than others."

The new draft constitution states in Section 56:3 that, "Every person has the right not to be treated in an unfairly discriminatory manner..." But then in Section 56:5 it says, "Discrimination on any of the grounds listed in subsection 3 is unfair unless it is established that the discrimination is fair..."

It goes on in Section 72, regarding rights to agricultural land to say:

> *(2) Where agricultural land, or any right or interest in such land, is required for a public purpose... the land, right or interest may be acquired by the State by notice published in the Gazette... whereupon the land, right or interest vests in the State with full title with effect from the date of publication of the notice.*
>
> *(3)*
>
> *(a) no compensation is payable in respect of its acquisition, except for improvements effected on it before its acquisition;*
>
> *(b) no person may apply to court for the determination of any question relating to compensation, except for compensation for improvements effected on the land before its acquisition, and no court may entertain any such application; and*
>
> *(c) the acquisition may not be challenged on the ground that it was discriminatory in contravention of Section 56.*

The new constitution then refers to all white-owned land saying that:

(4) All agricultural land which –
(a) was itemised in Schedule 7 to the former
Constitution; or
(b) before the effective date, was identified in terms of
section 16B(2)(a)(ii) or (iii) of the former Constitution;
continues to be vested in the State, and no compensation
is payable in respect of its acquisition except for
improvements effected on it before its acquisition.
(5) As soon as practicable after agricultural land is
acquired in accordance with subsection (2), the officer
responsible for the registration of title over land must,
without further notice, effect the necessary endorsements
upon any title deed and entries in any register for
the purpose of formally cancelling the title deed and
registering the State's title over the land.
(6) An Act of Parliament may make it an offence for
any person, without lawful authority, to possess or
occupy agricultural land referred to in this section or
other State land.

These clauses go directly against the SADC Tribunal Judgment of November 2008, and yet all legislators have agreed with it.

The Americans have much to teach us about property rights. Like Zimbabwe, America was a British colony. Like Zimbabwe, America got independence from Britain. Like Zimbabwe, America was primarily an agricultural country. Unlike Zimbabwe, America grew to be a prosperous country and the largest economy in the world in 129 years of independence. So what did America do with its independence which Zimbabwe has not understood?

America recognized certain fundamental principles that could not be altered. It recognized that men are created by God as equals in terms of their rights, with equality under the law being the basis for every good law made by man. They recognized that laws that favour privilege and therefore discriminate against others go against God's law and all notions of justice. America recognized that, regardless of who they are, individuals should have the freedom, through their own striving for excellence, hard work, thrift, and business acumen, to thrive and prosper – and indeed they have a duty to do so, for the good of their families and the wider community. America recognized that when governments take away this freedom through discriminatory laws, redistributive taxation, and a refusal to allow people to own property, they take away the individual's will to prosper.[11]

John Locke profoundly influenced American culture. Writing at the time of the Glorious Revolution in England, he argued "that being all equal and independent, no one ought to harm another in his life, health, liberty or possessions."

> *The reason why men enter into society is the preservation of their property… [Therefore] whenever the legislators endeavour to take away and destroy the property of the people, or to reduce them to slavery under some arbitrary power, [the officials of government] put themselves into a state of war with the people, who are thereupon absolved from any further obedience, and are left to the common refuge which God hath provided for all men against force and violence.[12]*

> *The Supreme power cannot take from any man any part of his property without his own consent. For the preservation of property being the end of government, and that for which men enter into society, it necessarily supposes and requires that the people should have property…[13]*

Though the earth and all inferior creatures be common
[as the gift from God] to all men, yet every man has
a "property" in his own "person." This nobody has
any right to but himself. The "labour" of his body and
the "work" of his hands, we may say are properly his.
Whatsoever then he removes out of the state that nature
hath provided and left it in, he has mixed his own
labour with it, and joined to it something that is his
own, and thereby makes it his property...[14]

Along the sides of the roads during the rainy season in Zimbabwe there are always people selling mushrooms. The mushrooms pop up with the rain, and the people go and find them and then stand by the road hoping that a passing motorist might stop to buy them. When the mushrooms were growing in the bush, they were the property of nobody. After they have been found and picked – sometimes after a long hunt – they become the property of the person who has found and picked them. There would never be any thought that the passing motorist would argue that the mushrooms are the common property of all Zimbabweans and therefore the seller must share them and give him some for free. The seller, by dint of using his time and energy to walk around collecting them, and then to stand by the road selling them, has gained ownership of the mushrooms. When the buyer gives him money the buyer then becomes the owner.

Similarly, even on communal land, nobody would think of demanding someone else's crops that they have spent their time, energy, and capital in cultivating – despite their being on land that is communal.

So when gangs come around to private land and the State allows them to take a farmer's crops it goes against all common customary law. One of the hardest things I ever had to endure was to watch, for day after day, while we lived in the house we had built a decade previously as Minister Shamuyarira's men used tractors, trailers, diesel, and harvesters that were the property of Mike Campbell Private Limited to reap crops that Mike Campbell Private Limited's capital, time, and energy had prepared the land for – planted, irrigated, fertilized, weeded, and sprayed.

I once caught some mango thieves who were operating from the neighbouring farm in a commercial theft consortium. It was a large farm village with over 1,000 people living there. During the daytime only the unemployed people were left in the village, along with all the children of pre-school age. They were a rough lot, many of them working in illegal gold mining nearby at Gadzema. At harvest time they would steal crops on a commercial scale. Among the labyrinth of huts we discovered one that was full of sacks of mangos stolen from the Mount Carmel orchards. They were waiting to be collected by pick-up. While my father-in-law went to try to persuade the police to come out, I waited in their farm village to make sure that they couldn't move the mangos.

I knew it was going to be a long wait and it was hot. The thieves were many and they realized that I was serious about waiting by the hut. Eventually, a few of the more desperate ones tried to manhandle me away from where I was waiting. There was an old iron fence pole stuck in the ground close by and, on perceiving their plan, I managed to work my way towards it and anchor myself with both hands while a few men tried to tear me away. The fence pole was not going to move, I was very determined to hang on, and they realized after some time that, unless they started to assault me with weapons, I was not going to be prised off it. The more they tried to lever me away from my anchor, the more tenaciously I clung onto it. Eventually, I hit upon the idea of calling the whole village around me and telling them a story.

"Once upon a time," I said, rather breathlessly for I had exerted a lot of energy clinging to my post, "there was a little red hen…" I proceeded to tell them, in a very long, drawn out way with lots of clucking noises and absurd actions, the nursery story about the little red hen who had ploughed the ground, planted the wheat, watered the wheat, weeded the wheat, harvested the wheat, ground the wheat, made it into dough, heated the oven, and baked it into a loaf of the most delicious bread… while the dog and the cat refused to help her. I had the village fascinated by the story – much of which was done in mime so that children could understand. At the end, I asked them whether the dog and the cat had a right to eat that bread.

In the middle of my story there was a great commotion as the thieves ran in the open, dragging fertilizer bag after fertilizer bag full of mangos. They managed to spirit them away to another hut some way away, so that when the police came it would have required a search of the whole village to find them. They knew the police would not institute a search. Needless to say, the consortium was allowed to continue their theft and the decent people were too afraid to expose them. They knew what would happen to them if they did. People living in lawless community do not last when they buck the system of institutionalized fear.

The great legal scholar, Sir William Blackstone, writing in England just before Locke about the natural rights of man, wrote that they "may be reduced to three principle or primary articles: the right to personal security, the right of personal liberty and the right of private property".

He said that the Creator's law was "dictated by God Himself" and is "superior in obligation to any other. It is binding over all the globe, in all countries and at all times; no human laws are of any validity if contrary to this…"

Another great thinker along similar lines was a Frenchman named Frédéric Bastiat. He wrote, in a book entitled simply *The Law*, while trying to stop "legalised plunder" by the State that:

We hold from God the gift which includes all others.
This gift is life – physical, intellectual and moral…
But life cannot sustain itself alone. The creator of life

has entrusted us with the responsibility of preserving,
developing, and perfecting it. In order that we may
accomplish this, He has provided us with a collection of
marvellous faculties. And He has put us in the midst of
a variety of natural resources. By the application of our
faculties to these natural resources we convert them into
products, and use them. The process is necessary in order
that life may run its course… Life, faculties, production
– in other words, individuality, liberty, property – this
is man. And in spite of the cunning of artful political
leaders, these three gifts from God precede all human
legislation, and are superior to it… Life, liberty and
property do not exist because men have made laws. On
the contrary it was the fact that life, liberty and property
existed beforehand that caused men to make laws [for
the protection of them] in the first place.[15]

Justice George Sutherland of the US Supreme Court told the New
York State Bar Association in 1921 at their annual address that,

the individual – the man – has three great rights,
equally sacred from arbitrary interference: the right
to his life, the right to his liberty and the right to his
property… The three rights are so bound together as to
essentially be one right. To give a man his life but deny
him his liberty is to take from him all that makes his
life worth living. To give him his liberty but take from
him the property which is the fruit and badge of his
liberty is to still leave him a slave.[16]

Abraham Lincoln once said:

Property is the fruit of labour. Property is desirable, is
a positive good in the world. That some should be rich

*shows that others may become rich and hence is just
encouragement to industry and enterprise. Let not him
who is houseless pull down the house of another, but let
him work diligently to build one for himself, thus by
example assuring that his own will be free from violence.*[17]

Without property rights three things occur:

1. Incentives to develop, improve, and produce on property evaporate.
2. Marauding bands invade property and thereafter asset-strip the good things that have been built up.
3. People live at a bare, subsistence survival level, because the accumulation of property invites jealousy, covetousness, and then invasion.

John Adams, one of the founding fathers of America had this to say:

*The moment the idea is admitted into society that
property is not as sacred as the laws of God, and that
there is not a force of law and public justice to protect
it, anarchy and tyranny commence. Property must be
secured or liberty cannot exist.*[18]

James Madison, another American founding father and US president, stated that:

*Government is instituted to protect property of every
sort... This being the end of government, that alone is
not a just government... nor is property secure under it,
where the property which a man has in his own personal
safety and personal liberty is violated by arbitrary
seizures of one class of citizens for the service of the rest.*[19]

Dr Ludwig von Mises, one of the world's foremost economists, wrote:

> *If history could prove and teach us anything, it would be the private ownership of the means of production is a necessary requisite of civilization and material well being. All civilizations have up to now been based on private property. Only nations committed to the principle of private property have risen above penury...*[20]

Christians are obliged to stand up and speak out for righteousness when the highest law of the land goes against God's law. In Zimbabwe I have not yet heard of one church that is doing this regarding property rights. Mugabe's propaganda has been so forceful that it would not be politically correct to raise the issue of the seizures as theft.

4

THE FORCE OF FEAR AND THE POWER OF LOVE

Tyrannical control has always been achieved by tyrants by playing on the minds of their subjects with lies and fear. In the vehicle of a brutal dictatorship, fear is the petrol that keeps the engine going. Fear levels among the people have to be continuously "topped up" to a high level, until living in fear becomes a conditioned way of life. The dictator tips the scales so that the cost of any action taken against him far outweighs the potential benefit.

On 26 January 2007, I received a call regarding the arrest of eight pastors from the Christian Alliance who were beginning to speak out at various churches around Zimbabwe. I immediately drove down to Kadoma where they had been put in jail. Other pastors from the Christian Alliance started to arrive. People gathered from all over Kadoma to show their solidarity. There was a huge movement of concern and righteous anger spontaneously manifest. The police were clearly very nervous. Pastor Chris Anderson from Gweru went to the supermarket and bought some bottled water for the pastors and asked if the police would give it to them. The duty officers shrank back in fear and didn't want to touch it. "This is holy water!" they exclaimed. They were clearly convicted about the wrong they were committing in arresting the pastors. They thought that something awful might befall them if they touched the "holy water".

There were suggestions that we should call other Christians to surround the police station to pray and sing. Then, the Baptist church building in Kadoma was offered to call a big prayer meeting, and there was general excitement about all coming together to pray. One of the leading pastors eventually spoke: "If we call a prayer meeting we will all get arrested too and we will not be of any help if we are all put in prison as well."

It was a critical moment. The other pastors wavered; the ardour dissipated. There was a general, reluctant agreement, and the moment was lost. After that everyone seemed to wander around looking rather directionless. There was an enthusiasm to try to make sure that the pastors were looked after and fed, but I could not help feeling that the fear of man, and the wisdom of the world, had spoken. God's wisdom in the situation had been lost.

Proverbs begins by saying, "The fear of God is the beginning of wisdom", and this message is repeated throughout the book. In Proverbs 29 we read that the "fear of man will prove to be a snare."

The pastors were released three days later on bail of 100,000 dollars (US$400) each. But after that, the Christian Alliance movement seemed to have a lot of the breath strangled out of it.

Just as the vehicle of brutal dictatorship has fear as its fuel, so Satan, the spiritual engine behind those who want power at any cost, wields fear as one of the greatest weapons in his arsenal. The protests in Zimbabwe are muted because everyone has been frustrated, disappointed, and browbeaten at every turn for so long. They are tired and afraid. The sense of outrage has been lost. It has been replaced by a latent passivity, and an all-pervading fear, which colours everything and everyone grey.

Fear is such an insidious thing. It creeps into our psyche without our even realizing it. It shapes our views, what we say, and how we act all the time – and most of us do not even know that it is happening. Fear is a shadowy, stealthy, evil force.

My uncle, who worked under Desmond Tutu as an archdeacon in Cape Town from the late 1970s to the early 1990s, spoke to the Anglican Church Synod in 2012 in a series of meditations in Bulawayo. He came away with an overwhelming feeling of the depth of the fear in the church in Zimbabwe. He did not feel there were any prepared to stand up and speak truth to those in power.

This is no surprise. Fear rules. Until the dark cloak of fear can be thrown off the people in countries where governments abuse their power, they will remain in bondage.

How do we dispense with fear though? Most church leaders, let alone their congregants, find it hard to admit they are governed by fear. Nearly nobody ever preaches about fear or how to overcome it. This is strange because, apart from the command to love, the command to not be afraid is the most repeated command in the Bible by a very long way.

Fear is the single biggest factor that allows tyranny to continue – and it will continue for as long as fear is allowed to reign.

As Christians, our first step to overcoming fear is to recognize it exists and then identify the source of the fear. What do we fear, and where does this come from? Is the fear rational or irrational? Is it physical fear or spiritual fear that requires moral courage and much prayer to counteract it?

When the eight pastors were arrested, there was clearly a great fear among many of the visiting pastors that they would be arrested too. They feared for their liberty; feared the shame of being in prison. Zimbabwean police cells are uncomfortable and cold, so they would be kept in horrible conditions. It was not so with those already inside. Pius Wakatama asked to be moved after twenty-four hours. "Why?" asked the police. "All those in my cell have become Christians and support the Alliance. I need a new congregation to work with," he said.

These prisons have become familiar to opposition activists, as well as to many farmers during the land invasions, shopkeepers in the days of price control, miners in the "clean-up" of mining, and so many others. Jenni Williams from the organization Women of Zimbabwe Arise has so far been in prison about fifty times. She and others in WOZA continue to be arrested regularly for "crimes" like giving out flowers during Valentine's Day marches.

Fear is something very real when the rule of law breaks down. When a government turns to brutality, people become afraid for their life, liberty, and property.

In 2012 I took a couple of people with me to Harare from a church we used to be part of. They told me that a relative of theirs had been beaten by the army and had died. His name was Jacob Kandange and he was a taxi driver. He was savagely beaten by the army along with a number of others. He managed to phone his wife to tell her what had happened and then started to stagger home. It took a few hours to get there because he had been so brutally beaten over the head and he was falling in and out of consciousness. It is amazing that Jacob got there. He fell down many times. He must have used all his willpower to get home to his wife and two little children. When he arrived home he was still able to speak and tell them what had happened, but then he lapsed into unconsciousness. In the morning he was still unconscious. His wife managed to get him to hospital. A little later he breathed his last. The doctor, in fear, recorded in his post-mortem that Jacob had fallen down while drunk and sustained head injuries, which had led to his death.

Trying to get more information was very difficult. I visited the place where his widow lived. It was a real slum. The flats had obviously been built quite well originally, but now the plaster was peeling and the walls had graffiti all over them. The windows were mostly jagged shards of angular, broken glass that seemed to cry out violence. I was amazed to see there was still running water. A leaking pipe had blackened a wall where it had obviously been running down for years, whenever the municipal water supply was working. There was rubbish lying around everywhere. I saw a child of about three or four walk by, barefoot in the rubbish with a soiled, faded red dress that was no more than a rag. She had a dirty plastic bag in her mouth. Overhead crows circled.

The relatives milled around. Some of them talked about the other people who had been beaten by the army at the same time as Jacob. However, nobody had made a report to the police. They were too afraid.

"We must pray about this," one of the relatives said. She was right. But then we must act, I thought. Does God not call us to overcome fear so that we can act?

I thought about what their fears could be – what all of our fears were. The people were afraid of suffering similar brutality at the hands of the authorities. They were afraid that they might be put in prison and deprived of their freedom. They were afraid that militia gangs might take their property if they were seen to be exposing the authorities. These are real fears that need to be overcome in situations where governments abuse their power.

The widow was on her way to Mutoko to bury Jacob's body. I made many offers of help over the phone. "If you allow them to get away with this what is to stop them doing it again, tomorrow, to the next person?" I asked.

She was not keen. She was afraid and didn't want to do anything to expose what the soldiers had done to her husband.

Psychologists have come up with thousands of fears that either motivate or demotivate people and dictate the actions that they choose to pursue. Ultimately there are only two fears: the fear of suffering and death on this earth, and the fear of God. The first fear is a negative fear; the second, a positive fear. The two fears work together to counteract each other. As the first fear grows, the second fear diminishes. As the second fear grows, courage surges up and we can become as brave as lions.

The fear of suffering and death is the biggest inhibiting power on earth. Mahatma Gandhi put it like this: "The enemy is fear. We think it is hate, but it is fear." Gandhi was referring to the first kind of fear. He did not truly know the liberating force of the second.

There are perhaps seven main fears we have that revolve around what others can do to us. Each relates in some way to how we can be manipulated by governments.

The Fear of Losing Our Lives

The first real fear is that our lives may be taken from us. In Zimbabwe, the death threat has been commonly used. Almost every opposition member, human rights activist, farmer, farm worker, or person who has been forced to a "pungwe"[1] has had to deal with this on many occasions. People from these groups have been strategically murdered or beaten in order to make everyone else terribly afraid. I described some of these murders in my book, *Mugabe and the White African*.

When people are afraid for their lives they are easily manipulated and silenced. Paul faced many threats to his life. He was able to overcome fear because he had total assurance in his Saviour. Shortly before his death, in prison in Rome, he wrote to the Philippians and told them that, "to live is Christ and to die is gain" (Philippians 1:21). He was able to mock death because he had total assurance of his eternal salvation. "Where O death is your sting? Where O death is your victory?" (1 Corinthians 15:55). As fellow Christians we need to know in our hearts what Paul knew.

The Fear of What Might Be Done to Our Family

The second fear is the fear of what a government can do to our family. When one's family is threatened, a person can be coerced very quickly into doing the bidding of an evil government.

In Nazi Germany, a law was passed in February 1945 that made any family member related to a person deemed not to have done his duty to the fatherland guilty of "Sippenhaft" or "kin liability". Families of soldiers who did not fight to the death would be deemed to be guilty of Sippenhaft. The brilliant German general, Erwin Rommel, when found to be part of the plot against Hitler, was given the choice of committing suicide or facing a people's court and being killed, with his family suffering and possibly being killed as well. He took the first option.

Above: When the masses were shouting "Heil!" what could the individual person do? You went along.

Right: Bodies of Jewish citizens being removed from an Iasi death train during the World War II pogrom in Romania.

Below: The gates of Auschwitz, the largest Nazi concentration camp, located in Poland (1945).

Above left: A Ukrainian Jew being shot by a Nazi killing squad [*Einsatzgruppe*] (1941).

Above right: Ceausescu's final speech in Bucharest before his arrest (1989).

Above: The detonation of Moscow's Cathedral of Christ the Saviour to make way for the Palace of the Soviets (1931).

Above left: Father Jerzy Popieluszko, murdered by Polish security police in 1984.

Above centre: Pastor Richard Wurmbrand, "tortured for Christ" in Romania; spent seven years in solitary confinement.

Above right: Pastor Dietrich Bonhoeffer was arrested for his staunch resistance to the Nazi dictatorship and hanged in 1945.

Above: László Tökés, who played an important role in the Romanian Revolution of 1989, receives the Truman-Reagan Freedom Award (2009).

Above left: Robert Moffat as a young missionary in South Africa (1795–1883).

Above right: Khama III (1837–1923), king of the Bamangwato people of Bechuanaland, now Botswana.

Above: (From left) Archbishop Dr John Sentamu, the Archbishop of York, Dr Paul Negrut, president of the Emmanuel University of Oradea in Romania, and Ben Freeth MBE, formerly of Mount Carmel farm and executive director of the Mike Campbell Foundation, at the launch of the foundation in 2012.

Stalin and Mao both used similar systems, victimizing families of people deemed to be part of any activity that went against the regime.

On one memorable occasion, the persecuted Romanian Pastor, Richard Wurmbrand, came to stay with my family, and I remember my mother telling me afterwards that she didn't know whether she would be able to resist the fear if her children were threatened. This was a fear that we were to face in Zimbabwe. At one stage, after a particularly terrible period of intimidation on the farm that lasted for many months, the thugs came round to our house at night shouting the threat, "We will eat your children!"

I remember Laura's grandfather telling me about his time on the run behind enemy lines after escaping from a prisoner-of-war camp. For a whole year he survived off the goodness of the Italian people. The villagers knew that if they were caught harbouring enemy soldiers they would all be killed in a collective punishment. To overcome such fear for the sake of a stranger is truly heroic. Laura's grandfather remained in lifelong contact with the people who had helped him.

The Fear of Physical Harm

The third fear that erring governments can instil is the fear of physical harm and pain. Such harm leaves a lasting memory and has far-reaching effects. Torture has been used down the ages to break people's spirits and bring them into line.

The most often used method of physical torture in Zimbabwe is the beating of the soles of people's feet. In the violence that surrounds elections in Zimbabwe this method of torture, known as *falanga*,[2] is used extensively. I have experienced it myself, and my father-in-law ended up with broken bones in his feet because of it. Peter Asani, the Mount Carmel farm foreman, is still in pain four years later, after having been tortured in this way. When we see the effects that physical harm has caused to others, it makes us very afraid of what might happen to us.

The Fear of Losing Our Property and Material Well-Being

Then there is the fear of the destruction or taking of our property and financial resources. In Zimbabwe, people have been allowed to steal or destroy all the property we have worked for. We have had our bank accounts seized, our pensions taken, our houses burnt, our household possessions looted or destroyed, farm machinery, crops, cattle, tractors, vehicles taken – all with absolute impunity. When the authorities allow theft on such a large scale, everyone becomes afraid. They believe that if they do anything that might be deemed to be standing up against the government, they will have the same thing happen to them.

The authorities in Zimbabwe have been very calculating in creating a public precedent for wide-scale looting. In 2001 we had the "Doma trashings", north-west of Harare. After a year and a half of violent invasions, where police refused to protect life or property, some farmers tried to resist a farm takeover by coming together to protect themselves against invaders. In the melee that followed, there were a few minor injuries on both sides. The farmers were immediately arrested, manacled, had their heads shaved, and were put in jail. Even a pastor coming to give them food received the same treatment. The invaders were allowed to walk free and continue with their invasions.

Then, in a period of four days, fifty-four farms were completely looted. Homesteads were stripped of furniture, curtains, pictures, family heirlooms, and all household goods. Security fences were rolled up and taken away. Plumbing pipes were taken out of houses. Whole roofs were taken off homes and spirited away. Window frames and doorframes were hacked out. Entire tobacco crops, all reaped, cured, and bailed up ready to go to the auctions, were carted off. Maize crops went the same way. Tractors and combine harvesters were vandalized. Overhead diesel tanks were broken open and the diesel allowed to run out like a river, swallowed up by the dusty ground.

Incidents were orchestrated to further instil fear. The Zimbabwe Broadcasting Corporation was brought in, and one man, Charl

Geldenhuys, who was hiding from the mob with his wife and young family in a strong room in his home, was accused by government ministers of shooting his own dog. They claimed that he was "being aggressive" towards those who were looting his property – and the looters were allowed to continue!

Some time later the government passed laws to allow the seizure of tractors, farm machinery, fertilizer, seed, chemicals, and other goods. No government budget was ever allocated for the "purchase" of these items, so people lived with the fear that their livelihood might be taken away at a moment's notice with no compensation. Of course, this fear became a reality for many people, including us.

The Fear of Incarceration in Prison

The fifth fear is the fear of incarceration in prison. When laws are made that allow for our arrest for doing nothing more than living in our own homes, it is easy to become very afraid. In 2002, when this happened and hundreds of farmers were arrested for living in their own homes, it caused widespread panic, and people packed up and left their homes. Some had been living there for three or four generations – and they were gone in twenty-four hours.

At the time of hyper-inflation in the economy, rather than stopping the printing of money and exercising strict financial discipline, applying policies that would encourage a productive economy, the government decided that to control inflation all it needed to do was enforce price restrictions and arrest any retailer caught exceeding them.

In a period of little more than a month 5,000 shopkeepers were arrested. The shelves emptied and nobody dared restock goods, knowing they would be forced to sell them below cost if they did not wish to find themselves in a dark, dirty, overcrowded cell and spend time sleeping on a concrete floor under a lice-infested blanket. Fear of arrest drove virtually the entire retail industry underground and onto the black market.

The Fear of Public Exposure of Our Sin

The sixth fear is the fear of public exposure of dark secrets – the skeletons in people's cupboards that they are fearful of being exposed. Secret agents are masters at luring people into compromising situations – either with money and material possessions or with "honey traps". Then the person who has succumbed is threatened with exposure, should they refuse to do their bidding. When people start to react to situations in a way that is out of character, it is a sign that this may have happened.

Our reputations are important to us. Archbishop Pius Ncube, the brave, outspoken Archbishop of Bulawayo, was ensnared in a "honey trap" with spy cameras in an extensive Central Intelligence Organisation (CIO) operation. There must have been debate within government circles as to whether to use the information to manipulate Archbishop Pius or simply to destroy his reputation immediately by public exposure. They must have realized that his convictions about the abuse of power by the government were too strong to silence while he was still in office. Therefore they decided to publicly expose and discredit him to get him out of office immediately.

The Spiritual Fear of the Dark Underworld

This seventh fear – of evil spiritual forces – is hard to define. It is perhaps the biggest demotivating force in Africa today. The fear of dead ancestors and malevolent spirits is something that is very real in some cultures. I was privileged to be brought up in a Christian home without superstition and spiritual fear, but that is not to say that I have not been subject to this fear and have seen it in others on occasion.

A leading Zimbabwean Baptist pastor, Ray Motsi, believes that one of the holds President Mugabe has on certain leaders throughout Southern Africa is based on fear of evil spirits. During the first "Chimurenga", or Matabele and Mashona rebellions in 1896, it was the spiritual leaders who were in charge, advocating the murder of all white people. Whole families, women, young children, and babies, were killed outright on the orders of spirit mediums. Over 10 per cent of the white population of Rhodesia was killed in this way in a period of a few weeks.

By the end of 1896, the Rhodesian authorities recognized the power of the spirit mediums behind the rebellion. Lord Earl Grey wrote to his wife, "Kaguvi is the witch doctor who is preventing the Mashona from surrendering." One of the native commissioners wrote, "If we capture Kaguvi the war is over." They were quite right. As soon as the spirit mediums were captured, the killing stopped immediately. Today such spirit mediums are revered by many in the current Zimbabwe government because of the ability they had to control people through fear.

Other Fears

There are other fears too. Some of them are irrational. Paranoia is able to creep into the psyche even where there is no sound reason to fear. Real fears engender a thousand false fears as the imagination starts to run and is not kept in check. The authors of fear are able to rely on this multitude of other fears. We are constantly vulnerable to the lies, deceit, and mind games fuelled by those who want us to live in fear so that we may be controlled. So often fear is based on falsehood masquerading as something real.

Often people have the fear of stepping out into the unknown. Where erring governments employ the use of fear so extensively it is always difficult to get people to discuss their fears openly and so take the first step towards confronting them.

I once took a seminar in Zimbabwe with a group of mostly poor black Christians where I had been asked to speak on the subject of overcoming fear. I read out the important text from Revelation 12:11 that says, "they overcame by the blood of the lamb, by the word of their testimony; and that they did not love their lives so much as to shrink from death."

I warned the people in the room that I would like to hear their own testimonies a little later. I then talked about the blood of the Lamb and about not shrinking from death and I gave a testimony of my own. During the break, I asked people to walk around outside, pray, and think about a testimony they might like to share of where fear had been overcome. Or, if the fear was still there, to share their fear so that we could pray for them.

When we resumed, there were almost no testimonies about overcoming fear, but also no discussions about what their fears were. People were too afraid even to bring up the things they were most afraid of. It was clear that their fears were so deep seated and overpowering that they could not even face them.

As long as this is the case and fear remains buried in the darkness within us, fear will continue to be effective in unjust rule.

Albeit under different circumstances, the American President Roosevelt put it well in his first inaugural address on 4 March 1933, at a time when America and the world was in a great economic crisis due to the Great Depression. He said, "The only thing we have to fear is fear itself – nameless, unreasoning, unjustified, terror which paralyses needed efforts to convert retreat into advance."

All of us at some time feel the "fear of man". However, if we allow it to master us, we will never be able to progress in life in a positive and constructive way.

If all these fears were distilled into three principle fears, they would be: fear for our lives, fear for our liberty, and fear for our property or possessions. Governments that do not protect life, liberty, and property are governments that are not carrying out their godly function and Christians need to get involved in challenging them.

I only became aware of the fear barrier a government will put up when I stumbled through it myself. The fear barrier is an invisible hedge surrounding every person who lives under tyranny and is therefore hemmed in by fear.

When we walk in fear, afraid of what a tyrannical government can do to us, all we see is that fear. We can't see how to get to a place beyond it. While we are hemmed in by fear, we are prisoners to it. All we see is colourless and grey; we see nothing beautiful or noble. Life becomes a dark, miserable thing because we live without hope. Love slowly dies in places that are so dark. Fear becomes a habitation. It stifles our passion, crushes joy and creativity, and slowly snuffs them out. We become filled with self-doubt, caution, and creeping cynicism, wizened grey men and women always looking furtively over our shoulders as though we are criminals. We come to reflect the spiritless place that encloses us.

The fears I have listed above are very real in oppressive dictatorships. They confront the people living within them at every turn. Like an old and broken nag we plod along the well-trodden, hemmed-in road, unable to loosen the reins and gallop wild and free. What we do not realize is that the place of freedom beyond fear is very close. We just need to break through the barrier to gallop on the sun-drenched plain beyond.

Biblical Responses to Fear

Paul writes in Romans 8:13–17:

> *For if you live according to the sinful nature, you will die; but if by the Spirit you put to death the misdeeds of the body, you will live, because those who are led by the Spirit of God are sons of God. For you did not receive a spirit that makes you a slave again to fear, but you received the spirit of sonship. And by him we cry "Abba, Father." The Spirit himself testifies with our spirit that we are God's children. Now if we are children, then we are heirs – heirs of God and co-heirs with Christ, if indeed we share in the same sufferings in order that we may also share in his glory.*

We learn here that fear is a spirit. This spirit of fear holds us in slavery if we allow it to be our master. Paul explains to us that as Christians we have a different master who is a loving Father. As a Father, he cares for us, his children. He loves us deeply and has made us his heirs. He has made us co-heirs with his Son, Jesus, who threw the stars into space, as we share in the same sufferings as him and those around us.

Paul writes again in 2 Timothy 1:6–7:

> *I remind you to fan into flame the gift of God, which is in you through the laying on of my hands. For God did not give us a Spirit of timidity, but a Spirit of power, of love and of self-discipline.*

He reminds us that the spirit of fear and timidity is not from God. The Spirit that we have been given to counteract fear is the Spirit of truth, manifested in power, love, and self-discipline. These things are the antithesis of fear. They cannot live together with fear. Paul instructs us to fan into flame the gift God has placed within us, so that fear is consumed by faith. Just as the oxygen from the bellows enlivens glowing coals to form a roaring fire with flames licking the wood, so the Spirit of power, love, and self-discipline will purge all fear.

Jeremiah wrote, "'Do not be afraid of the king of Babylon whom you now fear. Do not be afraid of him,' declares the Lord, 'for I am with you and will save you and deliver you from his hands'" (Jeremiah 42:11).

On the other side of the place called fear is a place called trust. It is located remarkably close to the place called fear and yet belongs to a different country, a different world even. As our faith grows, we come to trust our Father implicitly, like a sheep trusts a shepherd. The more we trust our Father, the more fear dissipates and begins to die. As we listen to the voice of the good shepherd, knowing that he is all-powerful and all-loving, we are miraculously led by him into this different world.

The key to breaking out of the place called fear that hems us in is placing our hand in God's hand. He provides the way out for us, if only we will follow the steps he prescribes. As we trust him and have faith in him, we are able to walk straight through the seemingly impenetrable fear barrier. If we falter though, if we take our eyes off the shepherd of truth, if we don't fan the flame within us, we will panic and scamper back to where we came from. It is only in the knowledge that God is all-powerful and all-loving towards us that we are able to move forward through fear.

When our family went to the SADC Tribunal to take on President Mugabe it was filmed by the world's media. The hook that brought the film crews out was the anticipation of what might happen next and the sense that this was a David and Goliath battle.

When David was a boy looking after his father's sheep, he rescued them from the mouths of lions and bears. He was able to find the courage to take on lions for the sake of the sheep he loved, which were under his care. We read that he even "grabbed the lion by the hair and struck it". David must have had a complete commitment to those sheep to risk his life and rescue them in such circumstances.

No one in the entire Israelite army was willing to fight the great Philistine giant, Goliath. But David, a teenage boy coming to the front line to bring his brothers some food, sized up the situation very quickly. David looked at the giant, so much bigger than he was, and listened to his boasts. He asked, who was this man that was allowed to "defy the armies of the living God"?

When his elder brothers ridiculed him as a mere boy, he did not lose heart. When he saw his brothers too frightened to stand against the giant, he did not allow the fear to be contagious.

David saw all the champions of the Israelite army, men much older, much bigger, and much better equipped than he was, in abject fear – but he did not succumb to the same fear himself. David knew that each of the mighty men in the king's army had the promise of wealth and even the hand of the king's daughter in marriage if they beat Goliath. Some of them were battle-hardened and strong, but they all "ran from [the giant] in fear". Yet David was unmoved in his resolve to take on his foe.

David approached King Saul – a tall, strong man himself – and was told by the king, "You are only a boy, and [Goliath] has been a fighting man from his youth." But David was still not deterred. He was not in awe of the king's words nor the king's lack of confidence in him.

We have to ponder, from where could David draw such confidence? The answer lies in the word itself. "Confidence" is from the Latin *con fides* meaning "with faith". David was supremely confident because he knew how God had helped him in previous fights with the lion and the bear. He had such confidence that God would use him to fight Goliath that he even rejected the king's armour. The boy decided to go out dressed just in the clothing of a shepherd boy with no more than a sling, a stone, and his faith. David was able to see this great Goliath and hear his taunts and still remain openly confident: "You come against me with sword and spear and javelin. I come against you in the name of the Lord Almighty."

David knew that it was not himself he had to trust. His trust was in the Lord Almighty – the one who is "almightier" than the biggest giant.

Even in the face of the giant's threats, taunts, and mockery David was still confident. I love the verse that says, "David ran quickly towards the battle line to meet him." This young teenager ran defiantly towards Goliath and the whole Philistine army, with the entire strength of the Israelite army cowering behind him, shrinking back. Even though the true, towering stature of the giant would now be apparent to David, he remained undaunted. He ran straight towards the fear and took it on. David trashed the hedge of fear that could have hemmed him in. Then he was out on the other side, in the glorious, open vista beyond.

Worldly wisdom would have taught him not to take on lions and bears when he was looking after the sheep. Worldly wisdom would have reasoned, "lions and bears will kill you, and then who will look after the sheep? Better stay clear. At least you can look after the sheep that are left after the lion has taken one or two." Similarly, worldly wisdom would have told him: "There are much stronger, better equipped men than me to take on Goliath. It's better that I don't get involved. I'll just return to my sheep. Even if the Philistines win, perhaps I can preserve my life and survive out in the hills with the sheep, as I have always done."

David did not listen to worldly wisdom. He overcame fear and won.

To go through the hedge of fear only takes three steps of truth:

1. The first step is to trust God. We trust in his character, that he is Almighty, all-loving towards us, and will not allow us to be tested beyond that which we can bear.
2. The second step of truth is to identify and expose the fears that are trying to war against our trust in Almighty God. We must replace them with a childlike faith in our all-loving Saviour through prayer and praise of our Almighty God.
3. The third step of truth is to walk – even to run – confidently towards fear, like David did, for the sake of others.

The apostle Paul tells us to put on our spiritual armour. He describes the belt of truth that holds both the breastplate of righteousness and the sword of the Spirit in place. The helmet of the truth of salvation must be firmly in place. The shield of faith must be used to deflect all doubt. The shoes of the truth of the gospel of peace must always be on our feet, so that we can travel through the stoniest deserts and the densest thorn thickets. Each piece of armour is designed for advance, not retreat. There is no armour on the back. It is not designed to protect those who are running away.

When we face a tyrannical government that is abusing its people we need to face the fears and doubts of what could happen to us and continue to blow the whistle, pointing to the truth despite our fears. We cannot remain silent. We must, in truth, "speak in the daylight... proclaim from the roofs" (Matthew 10:27). The things that defy God's law, his principles, and his ways must be brought into the public eye for all to see: lies, corruption, murder, theft – all need to be brought into the light and confronted. We need to help the victims and expose the perpetrators, using the law to try to seek justice. We cannot allow fear of "those who kill the body but cannot kill the soul" to stop us doing the things we know to be right.

The truth of the eternal perspective is so critical: life is very short and whatever happens we must do what is right and we must do it now. In the UK, the parting words "good bye" have become "stay safe"! But as Christians, our aim in life is not to live cautiously and make our way safely to our graves. Neither is it to store up material wealth to cushion us from difficulty. Life is short and we can take nothing with us, so we must focus on working out our eternal salvation. Life lived with an eternal perspective does not live for self-gratification. Neither does it live in fear of death or of what we can lose in this life. Rather it looks forward in confidence to what lies before us – a life lived in glory in the presence of Almighty God. Living for God and his kingdom changes our perspective completely. Fear falls away. It is not a "stay safe" existence that we choose when we choose Jesus. The apostles and the believers in the early church did not preach Jesus because they wished to "stay safe". They were put in jail. They lost their property. They were beaten. They were killed.

It did not stop them! Their perspective was much bigger, much higher than the here and now. They "learned the secret of being content in any and every situation" (Philippians 4:12). They were not bound and stifled by the fears of this earthly life.

To know the truth of the love and power of God and the promises that he has made to us transports us into a different place. It transforms us into different people because we find ourselves in another world, where new panoramas open up in front of us. When Paul said "to live is Christ and to die is gain", he had grasped the truth of "how high and how wide and how deep" is the love of God for us. He had accepted that love. He experienced that love so that it filled his being and there was no room for fear. Fear was driven out. "Perfect love drives out fear."

5

GODLY PEOPLE WHO OVERCAME FEAR AND SPOKE TRUTH TO POWER

The heathen Queen of Sheba rightly defined the role of government as "to maintain justice and righteousness" (1 Kings 10:9). Whenever kings in the Bible did not do this, God raised up people to challenge them.

There are many stories of godly men overcoming fear and defying the authorities and their unjust rule. These are recorded in the Bible for our inspiration and enlightenment.

There were the midwives who refused to obey Pharaoh and kill the baby boys because "they feared God and did not what the king had told them to do" (Exodus 1:17). God raised up Moses who defied Pharaoh and led the Israelites out of Egypt and slavery. Othniel was raised up by God to deliver the Israelites from the foreign King of Aram, who Othniel "overpowered" (Judges 3:7–11). Ehud was raised up by God to deliver the Israelites from the King of Moab, which he did by plunging a short sword into the king's obese stomach (Judges 3:12–30).

Then there were Deborah and Barak, who were raised up against King Jabin of Canaan, and Jael, who drove a tent peg into the head of the enemy General Sisera (Judges 4). Gideon was raised up by God to defy the Midianite oppression in the land (Judges 6–8). A woman armed with a millstone killed Gideon's tyrant judge successor, Abimelech (Judges 9). Jephthah delivered the Israelites from the Ammonites (Judges 10–12). Samson was raised up to defy the Philistines (Judges 13–16).

The list goes on. Samuel removed the blessing from King Saul when he did not follow God's commands (1 Samuel 16). David defied King Saul by not surrendering to him (1 Samuel 19). The guards and the officials defied King Saul by disobeying orders to kill the priests from Nob led by Ahimelech, because they knew they were innocent (1 Samuel 21). The "man of God" confronted King Jeroboam and shrivelled up the king's hand (1 Kings 13). The prophet Ahijah spoke God's words of judgment on King Jeroboam's wife (1 Kings 14:6–16).

The prophet Jehu confronted King Baasha about his sin (1 Kings 16). Elijah confronted King Ahab and Queen Jezebel and the prophets of Baal on a number of occasions (1 Kings 17–18). Naboth defied the king, refusing to sell his family vineyard to him (1 Kings 21). Elijah confronted the wicked King Ahaziah and his troops and they were burnt up; the king died. Jehu son of Nimshi was anointed by the prophet Elisha as the one who would fulfil God's judgment for what had happened to Naboth and confronted King Joram for the idolatry and witchcraft he was continuing to practise with his mother, Jezebel. Afterwards he shot the king between the shoulder blades with an arrow as well as killing King Ahaziah of Judah, Queen Jezebel, Ahab's family, and the prophets of Baal (2 Kings 9 and 10)! The priest Jehoiada ordered the murderess Queen Athaliah, the daughter of Ahab and Jezebel, to be taken out of the Temple and put to death (2 Kings 11).

There is no shortage of examples of people standing in God's power against the kings who ruled Israel and Judah whenever those rulers rejected God and followed paths of unrighteousness and injustice. Similarly, Peter exhorts us to "obey God rather than man" (Acts 5:29). The Bible commands governments to act justly and it consistently condemns the perversion of justice by rulers.

The prophets were raised up by God to speak truth to those in power. Obadiah spoke judgment on Edom; Amos spoke judgment on King Jeroboam and the priests; Nahum spoke doom on Nineveh and Assyria; Zephaniah spoke judgment on Judah and another five kingdoms; Jeremiah spoke judgment on Jerusalem and prophesied against at least nine other kingdoms; Ezekiel prophesied against another nine; Isaiah denounced thirteen kingdoms; Micah prophesied judgment on the leaders.

Many of the prophets suffered intense persecution for their forthright messages about the truth of justice and righteousness. They were abducted, tortured, imprisoned and killed for speaking the truth to power. But they overcame their fear and did not stop speaking out.

Daniel, Hananiah (renamed Shadrach), Mishael (renamed Meshach), and Azariah (renamed Abednego) were four men who overcame fear and stood up for God in a heathen land. They were all exiled to Babylon from Judah as boys with the rest of their people. Despite being renamed with ungodly names, incorporated into heathen Babylonian culture, and taught by heathen teachers, they remained faithful to God. They were cemented in their resolve to stand firm for the Lord and his truth, come what may.

As young boys, Daniel and his three young friends showed much promise, so they were set apart to be educated by King Nebuchadnezzar's officials. From the start they refused to be defiled by the king's food, to the extent that the king's official, charged with looking after them, was afraid he would be executed for neglect. But the boys were adamant in their stand to only eat in a godly way, and they did not waver.

When Daniel became a man, he was recognized as a person of integrity and administrative capacity. By the time he rose to be one of the three most important men in the kingdom, Babylon was the largest empire the world had ever seen. It stretched from the Indus River in India to the Mediterranean Sea and included present-day Turkey. When one of King Nebuchadnezzar's wives, the Princess of Media, became homesick for the mountains, he built the hanging gardens of Babylon (one of the seven ancient wonders of the world) for her on one of the palace roofs. These four young Jews were serving under a very powerful king.

When the king had a dream, it was Daniel who interpreted it. The king's dream was about a statue with a gold head, its chest and arms of silver, its belly and thighs of bronze, and its feet of clay mixed with iron. In the dream a rock carved from a mountain – the future millennial kingdom – smashed the statue.

The king must have thought about this, considering that the "golden head" represented his kingdom. Like all vain kings he wanted his kingdom to last forever, so he built a ninety-foot-tall statue made of gold from head to foot. Through God, Daniel had interpreted the king's dream, but the king had decided to defy God with this "image". The statue was presumably of himself, though the text is not explicit.

When the time finally came for all the people to gather in front of this magnificent image on the plain of Dura, everyone was ordered to "fall down and worship the image of gold" (Daniel 3:5) and warned, "Whoever does not fall down and worship will immediately be thrown into a blazing furnace" (v. 6).

It must have been a difficult decision for Shadrach, Meshach, and Abednego to refuse. Anyone of any consequence in the kingdom would have been present at this event (except Daniel, who was presumably busy keeping the king's affairs in order elsewhere). If the young men refused to bow down, they would stand out all too clearly. The power of crowd psychology is huge and to decide to defy it is difficult. They held positions of power. They knew that if they defied the king he would strip them of everything and they would suffer the death penalty. Little voices inside their heads must have cried, "No! For the sake of our survival and the good we can do in the future, we'll bow down, just this once." Human wisdom says, "Don't be stupid. Bow down. You're not harming anyone. It's not worth losing your life over. It's not worth threatening the future of your people by refusing to do this little thing." But human wisdom is not God's wisdom. They didn't do that. Instead, they overcame fear and openly defied the king's decree.

They were summoned by the furious king and asked whether it was true that they had disobeyed him. They replied:

> *O Nebuchadnezzar, we do not need to defend ourselves before you in this matter. If we are thrown into the blazing furnace, the God we serve is able to save us from it and he will rescue us from your hand, O king. But even if he does not, we want you to know O king, that we will not serve your gods or worship the image of gold you have set up.* (Daniel 3:16–18)

They were unwilling to compromise, even unto death. They were categorical in their answer. They understood that God's law superseded the king's. They did not even have to defend themselves. They knew that God would not necessarily rescue them, but that even if he didn't, they would still obey his law rather than the king's. They knew that to please God was far more important than to please man – even if it meant death.

It must have been a precarious moment for the king. He had all the leaders of his kingdom in front of him. He had the golden image symbolizing the perpetuation of his kingdom and wanted everyone to worship it. The expense of making it must have been a project every bit as big as the hanging gardens of Babylon. Now he had these three troublesome young Jews openly defying his decree. He worked himself into a rage. He ordered that the furnace be heated seven times hotter than usual. It was so hot that the soldiers throwing the young men in were burnt to death. When the boys were in the furnace, the miracle happened. A fourth man appeared visibly for all to see. The ropes that bound them were burnt away, but Shadrach, Meshach, and Abednego were able to walk around inside that terrible, blazing inferno with this fourth man, unharmed. When they came out they did not even smell of smoke. They were clean, untainted, and free.

"They trusted in [God]," the king marvelled, "and defied the king's command and were willing to give up their lives rather than serve or worship any god except their own God" (Daniel 3:28).

These three young men show us what overcoming the fear of tyrants is all about. We must trust in the "fourth man" who can bring the freedom from the things that bind us.

Givemore Maposa, a messenger at the Commercial Farmers' Union (CFU), with whom I'd maintained contact, told me months after our abduction, that the image of Shadrach, Meshach, and Abednego in the fiery furnace had immediately come into his mind when he heard Mike and Angela and I had been taken. Because of this, he said, he knew God would protect us.

When Daniel was in his forties he interpreted another dream of King Nebuchadnezzar's. He told the king that "your kingdom will be restored to you when you acknowledge that heaven rules". He went on to risk his position, his well-being, and his life by calling this proud and powerful king to repent and do justice in his land: "Therefore O king, be pleased to accept my advice: renounce your sins by doing what is right and your wickedness by being kind to the oppressed" (Daniel 4:27).

After a very troubled few years during which the king was mightily humbled and went out of his mind, he eventually did repent. He said, "I, Nebuchadnezzar praise and exalt and glorify the King of heaven, because everything he does is right and all his ways are just. And those who walk in pride he is able to humble" (Daniel 4:37).

Neither did Daniel hold back when rebuking Belshazzar, the next king of Babylon. By now Daniel was in his eighties. The seventy years of exile in Babylon were all but finished. At a feast a supernatural "hand" – the hand of God – wrote a message to the king. Daniel was called to interpret the words: *"mene, mene, tekel, parsin"*.

Before he did so, Daniel openly reminded the king of the wrongdoing of King Nebuchadnezzar before him and the fear and dread he had imposed on the people. Daniel told the king: "all the peoples and nations and men of every language dreaded and feared him. Those the king wanted to put to death he put to death; those he wanted to spare he spared..." Then, before the whole assembly, Daniel again spoke truth to power, knowing that his life hung in the balance because he was not saying things that this powerful king wanted to hear.

> *But you his son, O Belshazzar, have not humbled yourself though you knew all this. Instead you have set yourself up against the Lord of heaven. You had the goblets from his temple brought to you, and you and your nobles, your wives and your concubines, drank wine from them... you did not honour the God who holds in his hand your life and all your ways. Therefore he sent the hand that wrote the inscription. This is the inscription that was written: Mene, Mene, Tekel, Parsin. This is what these words mean:*
>
> *Mene: God has numbered the days of your reign and brought it to an end.*
>
> *Tekel: you have been weighed on the scales and found wanting.*
>
> *Peres [Parsin]: your kingdom is divided and given to the Medes and the Persians.* (Daniel 5:22–28)

Unbeknown to the king an invasion was in progress at that very moment. The city was about to be attacked. The course of the Euphrates River had been diverted so that the army of Darius could go under the city gates that spanned the river. We read, "that very night Belshazzar, king of the Babylonians, was slain" (Daniel 5:30).

The new king, Darius, appointed Daniel to be one of the three heads of his kingdom. One hundred and twenty satraps or governors were under him. Daniel once again distinguished himself as a very able administrator with his "exceptional qualities", and the king set him in place as the man in overall charge of the kingdom.

There was jealousy among the other senior administrators, so they tried to find areas where Daniel had been corrupt or negligent. But they could find no fault in him. Eventually, they decided that the only way to "fix" Daniel was to make a law that for thirty days no one could pray to any god but the king. They persuaded the king to put the law in writing – which meant not even the king himself could repeal it.

Like Shadrach, Meshach, and Abednego, Daniel was not afraid to die. We read that after this law was made he went straight to his room and opened his windows towards Jerusalem. He faced towards Solomon's Temple, which had been built to house the holy Law of God, and "prayed giving thanks to his God, just as he had done before". He did not obey the king's law because that would mean disobeying God's greater law, breaking both the first and second commandments. He did not try to hide the fact that he was breaking the king's law. He consciously and defiantly went to pray to his God and give him thanks, even though he knew that he would be thrown to the lions. He was being obediently disobedient – quite prepared to die rather than stop praying to God or compromise by praying less conspicuously.

Martin Luther King Jr said, "No one really knows why they are alive until they know what they'd die for."[1] Daniel was prepared to die for the only thing worth dying for: doing what is right in God's eyes. He knew that even at the cost of his own life, he had to make a public stand for God against the king's law – despite it being a law that would last only thirty days.

Daniel was cast out and thrown into the lion's den with the king's words echoing in his ears: "May your God, whom you serve continually, rescue you."

He spent the whole night in the pit among the king's formidable lions. In the morning, when the king came to see whether God had rescued him or not, he was able to say: "My God sent his angel, and he shut the mouths of the lions. They have not hurt me because I was found innocent in his sight." The "fourth man" had appeared once more. We read that, "When Daniel was lifted from the den, no wound was found on him because he trusted in his God."

John Calvin writes in his commentary on Daniel 6:22, "For earthly princes lay aside all their power when they rise up against God, and are unworthy of being reckoned in the number of mankind. We ought rather to utterly defy than to obey them…"[2]

Through Daniel's faithfulness and honest trust in God, God saved him even from the mouths and claws of lions. God then set him up to "prosper" in his old age, when the exile was at an end. He died in the year that the altar was rebuilt in Jerusalem.

Another man who spoke truth to power was Jonah. God told him: "Go to the great city of Nineveh and preach against it, because its wickedness has come up before me" (Jonah 1:2).

Nineveh was on the Tigris River, about 800 km from where Jonah lived. The people of Nineveh were known for their extreme cruelty to prisoners of war. Jonah knew this, so when he was told to go and confront the people with their wickedness and speak out against what they were doing, he decided that the best course of action was to run away and go to Tarshish, near Gibraltar, 4,000 km in the other direction! We read that "Jonah ran away from the Lord." The last thing he wanted to do was to confront a murderous bunch of idolatrous heathens with their sin! He must have been very afraid.

Furthermore, the people of Nineveh were enemies of Israel, and Jonah did not want to see them saved in the first place. Rather, he wanted to see God judge them and sort them out once and for all! Thus he decided to "flee from the Lord".

Jonah knew that he was sinning. He knew that God would not approve. He had already told the sailors on the ship he took that he was running away from the Lord. When the great storm came he knew that it was God speaking through the driving wind and waves, telling him he was doing the wrong thing by not confronting the Ninevites with their sin. His shipmates asked him, "What should we do to you to make the sea calm down for us?" (v. 11).

"Pick me up and throw me into the sea," he replied "and it will become calm. I know that it is my fault that this great storm has come upon you" (v. 12).

Even in their desperation in the howling wind, with waves pounding the ship and threatening to sink it, the sailors were appalled at the thought of throwing an innocent man overboard. But the sea grew "wilder"; it was "raging". They had tried to make for the shore but it was impossible. They had no choice unless they were all to be lost. After making their peace with this God of Jonah's, who they were now terrified of, "they took Jonah and threw him overboard, and the raging sea grew calm".

From "the depths of the grave" in the dark and fetid belly of the whale, which had swallowed him, Jonah called for help. Jonah describes his situation graphically. He writes how God had

> *hurled me into the deep, into the very heart of the seas*
> *and the currents swirled around me; all your waves*
> *and breakers swept over me… The engulfing waters*
> *threatened me, the deep surrounded me; seaweed was*
> *wrapped around my head. To the roots of the mountains*
> *I sank down; the earth beneath barred me in for ever.*
> (Jonah 2:3, 5–6a)

There is no picture more desperate, no image of a man more completely alone and lost than Jonah in that raging, terrible tempest in the midst of the sea after he had refused to confront the Ninevites with their sin. No wonder Jesus referred to this incident. The Pharisees wanted a miraculous sign and Jesus exclaims, "A wicked and adulterous generation asks for a miraculous sign! But none will be given it except the sign of the prophet Jonah" (Matthew 12:39). Jesus was referring not just to the generation of his time, but to the generation in Nineveh that Jonah was unwilling to confront. Jesus was like Jonah, calling his contemporary "Nineveh" to repentance. Similarly, we must be prepared to confront all that is wicked in our generation. The call of Jesus and Jonah is upon us, to turn from our own wicked ways and call upon others – even the powerful rulers of nations – to do the same because of God's amazing grace.

Another man who stands out is Nathan.

One night, in the spring when his army was out fighting the Ammonites, King David went out onto the balcony of his palace roof and saw a "very beautiful" woman who was bathing by lamplight, probably in the courtyard of her house. He was transfixed by her, captivated at once, even though he had his own wife and a harem he had inherited from Saul. He discovered that Bathsheba was married to one of his loyal soldiers, Uriah. At this time David was in the heyday of his reign. Women swooned before him. He was like a celebrity in the land. He was man of passion and action. He should really have been at the battlefront, fighting, but here he was with time on his hands. He lusted after Bathsheba and, when he should have resisted, he went ahead and called for her to be brought to him. He allowed his passion to master him, they committed adultery together, and she conceived.

When David heard Bathsheba was pregnant he summoned her husband Uriah back from the battlefront. David tried to cover his sin up. If he could get Uriah to have sex with his wife, then Bathsheba could deceive him into thinking it was his own child. But, unlike David, Uriah was too principled and dedicated to his men. He wouldn't consider living it up at home while the rest of his troop was slogging it out on the battlefield. Even when David got him drunk he didn't go home.

David rethought. He was in deep trouble now. The whole situation was compounding. If he couldn't use deceit to cover up the secret of his sin, he would have to do away with Uriah altogether, he concluded. David's orders to his general were cold, calculating, and manifestly evil. "Put Uriah in the front line… then withdraw from him so he will be struck down and die" (2 Samuel 11:15). It was straightforward murder. David then took the wife of that faithful soldier he had had murdered to be his own wife.

Nathan the prophet came to confront him. He spoke the truth with great wisdom and told David a "story" about a certain man. He spoke of a rich man who had taken a poor man's treasured ewe lamb, so precious that it "even slept in his arms" and "was like a daughter to him". The rich man then had a visitor. Rather than slaughter his own lamb, he took the ewe lamb from the poor man – his only sheep – and ate that one instead. David was incensed. How could a rich man commit such an injustice against a poor man's treasured possession: "the man who did this deserves to die!" he declared.

> *Then Nathan said to David:"You are the man!… Why did you despise the word of the Lord by doing what is evil in his eyes? You struck down Uriah the Hittite with the sword and took his wife to be your own."* (2 Samuel 12:7–9)

David's confession and repentance was immediate, full, and sincere. He had broken all of the second half of the Ten Commandments. With a "broken spirit and a broken and contrite heart" (Psalm 51:17) he poured out to God. Though the consequences of his sin were dire, his prayer to "create in me a new heart, O God, and renew a steadfast spirit within me" (v. 10) was answered. The forthright words of truth spoken by Nathan directly to the king regarding his injustice, evil, and murder revived the king's heart. Nathan's courage in not remaining silent had led to the king's repentance and prevented his conscience from being seared. He would not become harder. Evil would be averted.

Emulating the courage of Nathan, there were various churchmen during the Nazi era who were not silent regarding the oppression of the Jews.

The Catholic cardinal, Michael von Faulhaber, the so-called Lion of Munich, said in October 1938, "History teaches us that God always punished the tormentors of... the Jews. No Roman Catholic approves the persecution of Jews in Germany." [3] His palace was fired upon by the Nazis for preaching against racism. Unfortunately, he did little to help the Jews because he felt, rather sadly, that any real protests would be "useless".

The Protestant church in Nazi Germany was far larger, comprising around 45 million of the 65 million German population. There was a focused attempt by Hitler to make it an organ of the State. He got his own man appointed who set about the complete Nazification of the Protestant church. By September 1933, the same year Hitler came to power, the synod incorporated the Aryan Paragraph in church law. This excluded Jews or people from a Jewish background from being part of the church. The Aryan Paragraph had already been incorporated without protest throughout public services, agriculture, the press, theatres, public health, and in almost all professions with no meaningful resistance.

Within five days, sixty pastors met on 11 September and signed a document rejecting the Aryan Paragraph as unchristian. Martin Niemöller was elected as president of this "Pastors' Emergency League". By the end of September, 2,036 other pastors had signed the document. By January 1934, 7,036 pastors had signed to reject the Aryan Paragraph.

In May 1934 many worried Protestant pastors met at Barmen and signed the Barmen Declaration, which declared that the church was not an organ of the State and that no human *Führer* could stand above the word of God. They refused to accept that the State could change their confession of faith. By that they became known as the "Confessing Church".

The Confessing Church soon found itself in principled opposition to many of the policies of the State. It was a time of great fear and change and initially no one was prepared to take the lead, reach consensus, and speak out.

In 1935, a Berlin deaconess, Marga Meusel protested about the Confessing Church's timid action:

> *Why does the Church do nothing? Why does it allow*
> *unspeakable injustice to occur?... What shall we one*
> *day answer to the question, where is thy brother, Abel?*
> *The only answer that will be left to us, as well as to the*
> *Confessing Church, is the answer of Cain.[4]*

Another respected theologian and instrumental member of the Confessing Church, Karl Barth, wrote in 1935, "For the millions that suffer unjustly, the Confessing Church does not yet have a heart."[5]

These voices of conscience had their effect. On 4 June 1936 the Confessing Church sent a polite but very bold, firm memorandum to Hitler protesting anti-Christian tendencies in National Socialism, denouncing racism and anti-Semitism in the Aryan Paragraph, and demanding a curtailment of interference with the affairs of the church. They questioned whether the chancellor was trying "to de-Christianize the German people". They went further in their memorandum to Hitler and challenged anti-Semitism on the basis that it went against a founding Christian command to love your neighbour:

> *When, within the compass of the National Socialist view*
> *of life, an anti-Semitism is forced on the Christian that*
> *binds him to hatred of the Jew, the Christian injunction to*
> *love one's neighbour still stands, for him, opposed to it.[6]*

It was a brave move. Hitler acted decisively and viciously: Seven hundred pastors were immediately arrested and put in concentration camps until the end of the war, including Pastor Martin Niemöller. They lost their properties. Their journal was banned. Their seminary was suppressed. The church, as the only corporate body prepared to stand against Hitler's programme of persecution, was left leaderless and severely mauled.

Albert Einstein was quoted in *Time Magazine* on 23 December 1940 as saying:

> *Being a lover of freedom, when the revolution came in Germany, I looked to the universities to defend it, knowing that they had always boasted of their devotion to the cause of truth; but, no, the universities immediately were silenced. Then I looked to the great editors of the newspapers whose flaming editorials in days gone by had proclaimed their love of freedom; but they, like the universities, were silenced in a few short weeks... Only the Church stood squarely across the path of Hitler's campaign for suppressing truth. I never had any special interest in the Church before, but now I feel a great affection and admiration because the Church alone has had the courage and persistence to stand for intellectual truth and moral freedom. I am forced thus to confess that what I once despised I now praise unreservedly.*

Hitler created a Ministry of Church Affairs to Nazify it. His Minister of Church Affairs spoke the lie on 13 February 1937 that, "positive Christianity is National Socialism... and National Socialism is doing God's will... the German people are now called by the Führer to a real Christianity... The Führer is the herald of a new revelation."[7]

Pastor Dietrich Bonhoeffer had not immediately been arrested. He wrestled with the theological question of what should be the

Christian response in times of intense persecution. Should he accept as truth what John Knox, the great Scottish Reformer, had said to Mary Queen of Scots in 1561: 'If monarchs exceed their lawful limits they might be resisted even by force"?[8]

Bonhoeffer became involved in a plot to try to rid Germany of the Nazi machine that was destroying everything in its path. He was quoted as saying,

> *If I see a madman driving a car into a group of innocent bystanders, then I can't, as a Christian, simply wait for the catastrophe and then comfort the wounded and bury the dead. I must try to wrestle the steering wheel out of the hands of the driver.[9]*

In the book of Job we read that Job did more than call for repentance. He "broke the fangs of the wicked and made them drop their victims" (Job 29:17). We are called to do this too in times of such tyranny. Bonhoeffer took these words seriously. Tragically, he was arrested in 1943 and martyred three weeks before Hitler committed suicide.

Other members of the Confessing Church got involved in the underground work of trying to assist Jews with forged identity documents, feeding and hiding them against the law. Unfortunately the Nazi system was fanatically efficient, and the fear was overpoweringly oppressive. There were not large numbers of Christians prepared to risk their lives for others, particularly after the Jews were put in the ghettos and were "out of sight". Of the 240,000 Jews in the ghettos of Nazi Germany and Austria when the killing began, only 7,000 survived the Holocaust.

In other invaded countries, there was more resistance from the church.

In May 1940 the Dutch clergy issued a joint protest in relation to the compulsory registration of the Jews. In June 1942, when Jews were forced to wear the yellow stars of David, Dutch

Christians wore yellow flowers on their clothes. The church made other protests, and the Nazis decided to negotiate. The Protestant church compromised to stop their protest if the deportation of Jews married to Gentiles and converted Jews were stopped.

The pastoral letter of February 1943 read: "Should the refusal of collaboration require sacrifices from you, then be strong and steadfast in the awareness that you are doing your duty before God and your fellow man."[10] Forty-nine priests were killed for helping the Jews.

Cardinal Jozef-Ernest Van Roey of Belgium was chastised by some for using his position in the church to speak out against the Nazi movement. When questioned on this he responded: "The hierarchic authority is perfectly entitled to pronounce on any political party or political movement in so far as that party or movement opposes religious well being or the precepts of Christian morals."[11]

Later he was more explicit: "We have a duty of conscience to combat and to strive for a defeat of these dangers [of Nazi Germany]... reason and good sense both direct us towards confidence, towards resistance..."[12]

His words and actions regarding the Jews being deported from Belgium in September 1943 had the effect of getting the deportations halted. The cardinal wrote, "It is forbidden to Catholics to collaborate in the formation of oppressive governments. It is obligatory for all Catholics to work against such a regime."[13] Those that were about to be deported were released. Of the 90,000 Jews in Belgium, including the 30,000 refugees, 65,000 survived the Holocaust.

In France, Bishop Kerkhofs of Liege ordered all his priests to assist the Jews. He hid a rabbi in his own home and when the Gestapo came knocking on his door, he put the rabbi in different clothes and introduced him to them as his "private secretary".[14]

In June 1942, when Jews were ordered to wear the yellow star of David, the bishops reacted by wearing yellow stars on their own robes. Other Christians wore yellow handkerchiefs in their breast pockets and carried bunches of yellow flowers. When 22,000 Jews were rounded up in Paris for deportation in mid July, Archbishop Saliège of Toulouse, Bishop Théas of Montauban, and Cardinal Gerlier of Lyon protested. The pastoral letter, known as the *Bombe Saliège* was banned, but it was still read out in some 400 churches.

Bishop Théas was arrested, but the French church was not deterred. Cardinal Gerlier, the French primate, in his pastoral letters urged French Christians to give Jews "every assistance". Adolf Eichmann ordered the French prefect of Lyon to arrest nine Jewish children that Cardinal Gerlier had been harbouring in his residence. When the prefect got there he found that the children were gone. "Tell me, to which address have they gone?" he demanded.

The cardinal replied, "Monsieur Le Prefet, I would not consider myself to be Archbishop of Lyon if I complied with your request. Good day."[15] He shut the door.

By the end of the war Father Chaillet, the cardinal's aide, had hidden and cared for 1,800 Jews in monasteries and on farms.

Although the Pope did not directly refer to the Jews, his Christmas message in 1942 spoke with sorrow and compassion of "those hundreds of thousands who, without any fault of their own, sometimes only by reason of their nationality or race, are marked for death or progressive extinction".

A pro-Nazi newspaper in Lyon lamented,

> *Every Catholic family shelters a Jew… Priests help them across the Swiss frontier. In Toulouse, Jewish children have been concealed in Catholic schools; the civilian Catholic officials receive intelligence of a scheduled deportation and advise a great number of the refugee Jews about it, and the result is that about fifty percent of the undesirables escape.[16]*

Right: The probable remains of a teacher who was severely beaten and then shot in Matabeleland South during Gukurahundi in 1984. Many bodies were thrown down mine shafts or buried in mass graves and thousands of people remain unaccounted for.

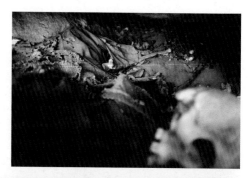

Above: In 1984, Alice's 32-year-old son was hung upside down by his feet from a branch of a tree and beaten to death by Prime Minister Robert Mugabe's North Korean-trained 5th Brigade. During the Gukurahundi era of 1983-87, some 20,000 civilians were murdered.

Left: During the horrific pre-Presidential election violence in Zimbabwe in 2008, Joshua Bakacheza, a Movement for Democratic Change driver, was abducted with a colleague by suspected State security agents. After being viciously tortured, Bakacheza was shot and killed. His body was dumped in the veldt.

Top: During the Zimbabwe government's Operation Murambatsvina, a ruthless campaign claimed to be "cleaning up squatter camps" in urban areas, even solid brick houses were torn down by State bulldozers. Churches worked tirelessly to provide food and shelter for the destitute.

Above: A young boy in the rubble of a demolished business centre south of Harare.

Left: A small child comforts a cold and terrified toddler after their home was destroyed during Operation Murambatsvina in May 2005.

Left: The body of commercial farmer Terry Ford, murdered on Gowrie Farm in the Norton district of Zimbabwe in March 2002 during the violent land seizures. His faithful Jack Russell terrier, Squeak, refused to leave his master's side.

Below: Crop failures have continued in the wake of the invasions and ongoing takeovers of Zimbabwe's highly productive commercial farms.

Right: A "Foundations for Farming" demonstration plot of maize (corn) in Chegutu.

Far right: In 2009, prisoners in Zimbabwe's jails were lucky to receive one meagre meal a day as food ran out. Charity organizations provided food, clothing, and drugs to prevent escalating deaths.

Above: Pius Ncube, the outspoken and fearless former Roman Catholic Archbishop of Bulawayo, led processions and church services to raise the profile of the widespread suffering in Zimbabwe. This demonstration of solidarity took place in Bulawayo on Good Friday, 25 March 2005.

Right: The crucifixion is where justice and mercy met. As Christians, we are commanded to take up our crosses as Jesus did to bring hope and justice in a lost and fallen world.

In 1943, 1,200 priests were arrested in a period of two months in France and deported. Father Pierre-Marie Benoit ran an extensive forgery operation in the cellars of the Capuchin monastery in Marseilles. Here he forged fake identity cards, baptismal certificates, and other documents for Jews. He organized evacuations twice a week to Spain and Switzerland. He risked his life, time and time again. When it was clear that the Gestapo were catching up with him, he moved to Italy under the name of Friar Benedetti and carried on his forgery mission there.

Pope Pius condoned these measures. The Vatican itself issued 6,000 Jews with passports and visas on papal orders. Of the 9,700 Jews in Rome, 5,000 were hidden by the church in monasteries and other church buildings, and a further 3,700 were hidden in private homes through the offices of Monsignor O'Flaherty. Only 1,007 were deported to Auschwitz.

In Hungary, after nearly half a million Jews were deported in less than three months from the end of April 1944, the Pope together with the Red Cross and King Gustav of Sweden protested and the deportations were stopped.

In Poland, where by far the biggest majority of the Jews in Europe lived, the persecution by the Nazi invaders was more extreme than anywhere else. Poland was the only country where the death penalty was introduced for non-Jews who dared to help Jews.

In some regions, 80–90 per cent of the priests were either killed or taken to concentration camps where 3,000 clergy perished. Even so, Archbishop Andreas Szeptycki of Lwow risked his life by hiding 21 Jews in his cathedral and 183 more in convents and monasteries. Other clergy and Christians followed his lead, and thousands of Jews were saved by these incredibly brave acts of mercy that cost many of the merciful their own lives.

All over Nazi-occupied Europe ordinary Christians risked their lives by looking after the Jews. Dr Gertrude Luckner, a German Roman Catholic social worker, when raided by the Gestapo and asked who was behind the operation that she was involved in, saving Jewish people from capture, replied: "My Christian conscience."

And so it must be with all of us who live in times where governments go against God's law.

As the Iron Curtain was drawn across Europe, a deep darkness descended in the east. Where the sun should have been casting its glowing rays at the end of the five years of the world at war, the red star flag of a godless ideology cast a deep shadow.

For a whole generation few chinks of light could be seen. There was a resignation by most that as individual pawns in the games of the great powers, they could only put their heads down and survive in the twilight world that had been created. By the next generation though, sparks were beginning to kindle in the minds of thinkers. They realized that if they wanted things to change, then as individuals they had to get involved and change them.

Lech Wałesa, the Polish politician, trade union organizer, and human rights activits, commented that, "The invocation of a moral order was the most revolutionary that could be made to an increasingly dogmatic socialism practiced in Poland, and people were caught up in the wave of moral reawakening..."[17] The Polish church emerged as a vibrant rallying standard for the people.

Just before Christmas 1970, food and fuel prices were hiked up in the control economy of Poland. At the Lenin shipyard in Gdansk, workers went on strike. Police intervened, but the workers' blood was up and there were violent clashes. The Polish army was sent in with tanks and machine guns. They opened fire on the workers and at least 28 were killed and over 1,000 injured. Several thousand more were arrested.

The church got involved. Priests helped to trace missing people and recorded secret burials at night. Afterwards, the workers welded up huge angular steel crosses out of pipes with bracing struts, making them into triangles. The sides symbolized faith, sacrifice, and solidarity. On the top were welded anchors – the wartime emblem of the home army. At the base were lines from the psalms. They erected them in the places where the workers had fallen.

As the pressure grew the price hikes had to be stopped, but the tide was turning. Economics was beginning to dictate the agenda. Marxism was failing to deliver what people needed in order to survive. Foreign debt was ballooning and soon hyper-inflation would be flooding Poland with Zloty. The first time I became a millionaire was in Warsaw in 1990 when I changed a few US dollars to buy a train ticket to Rotterdam. (In Zimbabwe I became a trillionaire many times over!) The economy was in ruins.

In 1977, Charter 77 was signed in Czechoslovakia by a number of so-called dissidents, including the playwright, dissident, and politician, Václav Havel, who became the first president of the Czech Republic. They decided to hold their government to account regarding the freedoms guaranteed by the international treaties that the government had signed. Another Czech, Václav Benda, said that it was vital to "shake that evil off, escape its power and seek the truth".[18] Behind the Iron Curtain an awakening to the truth was taking place.

In 1978 the first non-Italian Pope for centuries was chosen. At his installation the former Polish priest, John Paul II, finished with the words given by God to Joshua before crossing into the Promised Land: "Be not afraid." After forty years in the desert they were words Joshua needed to hear. They were also words that the people of Eastern Europe needed if they were to throw off totalitarian rule. The idea of a moral transformation involved shaking off the cloak of fear and trying to live life as if the oppression was not oppressive. In a sense, it was a kind of escapism to transport them to where they knew they wanted to be. If they could not walk through the wall that separated them from the free societies in the West, then they would bring what was beyond the wall to their oppressed societies in the East, merely by acting out the freedoms that they believed were the truth. By so doing, they were somehow walking through the wall – even demolishing the wall – in their psyches. Fear was being overcome in an organic, non-violent play.

As the acts went on, more and more players were inspired and became involved. Eventually, with almost the entire "audience" now on the stage, the curtain was torn down and the play mutated into the reality of truth. Totalitarianism was becoming obsolete. The totalitarian communist clique was gradually exposed for what it was: a tiny, predatory, quisling band of evil men attached to a foreign power sitting at the back of the theatre.

The regime did not know how to deal with non-violent protest. The new Pope, no friend of totalitarianism, switched the spotlight on. The regime could not just mow down unarmed people. The glare was too great and the economic consequences for those struggling Marxist economies, all left in the dust by the people across the divide in the free market West, would have been too dire.

In the summer of 1979 the Pope visited Poland. During his nine-day visit, 13 million people turned out to see him. There was a mighty hunger for God. People wanted God's justice and his truth and freedom in their land. At a mass in Victory Square in Warsaw the people responded with chants of, "We want God! We want God! We want God in the family circle! We want God in the books in schools! We want God in government orders! We want God! We want God!"[19]

One of Lech Wałesa's first acts as the chairman of the new Solidarity Movement of the Independent Trade Unions was to be photographed under a huge cross. There was a mass move of millions of Communist Party cadres to the Solidarity cause – and the cross.

Priests established relations with the workers. When martial law was declared close to Christmas in 1980, 3.5 million telephones went dead and 10,000 people were arrested and placed in internment camps. Tanks and armoured cars were positioned at all the intersections and the army took control.

The churches filled up, and the priests spoke bravely to the thousands about the need to resist the evils of the regime. With the Pope's visit in 1983, more impetus was added and Solidarity continued to gain ground. It was as though a mighty unstoppable wave had been formed.

One priest, Jerzy Popiełuszko, drew crowds of up to 15,000 at a time. In desperation, the regime decided that they needed to get rid of him. An orchestrated car crash failed, but in October 1984, security officials flagged him down and beat him to death, putting his body in a reservoir, and weighing it down with stones. The driver of the car was handcuffed but managed to make his escape.

At his funeral hundreds of thousands of people arrived to pay tribute to this brave speaker of truth. His grave became a Solidarity shrine and was the focal point for a mounting storm of internal pressure and international outrage. This forced the regime to arrest the captain and the other two agents of the security service who had killed Popiełuszko and bring them to trial.

The wave surged on and in 1989 the Solidarity Movement swept the totalitarian clique out into the cold. A free market economy was developed, and basic freedoms were established. The economy became the fastest growing in Europe, and Poland now has the twenty-first largest economy in the world.

I have the privilege of counting Pastor Paul Negrut from Romania as a friend. He told me about the wave of truth – in which he participated – that swept Romania's dictator Nicolae Ceaușescu from power. Various pastors wrote a joint letter to the president calling upon him to repent of the evil acts in which he had participated. The letter took a long time to write because they prayed over every word in order to get agreement. When they each signed the letter they knew that they were probably signing their own death warrants. They were aware of the terrible torture that Pastor Richard Wurmbrand and so many others had endured for their belief in Jesus Christ. A few days later the State church wrote a letter praising the dictator as a wonderful leader.

A large Christian gathering in the town of Timisoara had been organized with a speaker from outside. László Tökés, a Hungarian pastor who was part of the gathering, was warned that the secret police were going to arrest him, so rather than going into hiding, people came to surround his apartment and pray.

It is immensely powerful when this happens. I remember the last night that the Beatties, who had been subjected to appalling harassment, spent on their farm outside Chegutu. I was there with Tom and Sue's daughter, Sarah-Jane, and her husband Simon. Singing started up. I could tell immediately that it was not the forced *jambanja*[20] (all-night ZANU-PF indoctrination session) singing. It was most definitely church singing, with all the beautiful rich harmonies that come from African choirs. The singing started as the sun went down and as we lay half awake throughout that long night, one ear open listening for *jambanja* drums or the invaders to start looting the house, the singing continued. There was not a sound from the invaders to destroy the heartwarming comfort of the singing.

At first light, I looked out from an upstairs window and could see in the dawn a large, semicircular throng of people standing and facing towards the invaders and the house which we were in, beyond them. They were still singing. We went out, passing through the invaders whose fires were on the lawn, and thanked them. It was the farm workers wanting the white people to stay.

In Timisoara, where people had come to pray for László Tökés, very soon, large numbers had gathered and they were filled with the knowledge that God is alive. All through the night they prayed around his apartment. After some time they started to walk to the communist headquarters in their town to pray. Others joined in, many of them students. They began to chant, "God is alive! Down with the dictator!"

The dictator sent in the army. Pastor Paul Negrut and all the people continued to pray and chant, "God is alive! Down with the dictator!" and the army opened fire on them. Though it was

December and bitterly cold, the worshippers took off their shirts and waved them in the air to demonstrate how naked they were before the armour of the tanks.

The soldiers stopped shooting and joined them.

The movement snowballed into other towns. Eventually, on 21 December 1989, the dictator called a mass support meeting in Bucharest in the great square now known as Revolution Square. He stood on a balcony to address the crowds, many of whom he had brought in as his loyal supporters. A little while into his speech the crowd started chanting to drown him out. It developed a life of its own. He tried to speak but his voice was overpowered by the clamour from below: "God is alive! Down with the dictator."

He faltered and went back inside. He came out again to try once more, but the crowd of thousands of people shouted all the louder. He raised his right hand weakly, his face a picture of crestfallen surprise. He left the balcony again and took refuge inside.

His Minister of Defence, with the army refusing to act, committed suicide. It was thought at the time that he had been murdered by the dictator for refusing to send the army out. A wave of anger rippled through the army rank and file and the country as a whole. The dictator's army commanders abandoned him.

Ceaușescu made a last desperate attempt to address the crowd, but was bombarded with stones. His voice was drowned by the chanting. The Central Committee building was stormed, and he had to quickly board a helicopter he had waiting on the roof. The army ordered the helicopter down, and police arrested him. He was handed over to one of his elite paratroop units who "tried" him in a show trial, lined him and his wife up on Christmas Day, and shot them.

Miraculously, less than a month after the joint letter had been written by the pastors, the newspaper headlines read, "God is alive! The dictator is dead!"

6

JESUS AND THE LAW; INJUSTICE AND THE AUTHORITIES

Jesus experienced injustice in a fundamental way. As the most innocent man that ever lived he was condemned to suffer the most cruel and horrible death imaginable.

The injustice of Jesus' trial was manifold. There was no public notification. It was held in the middle of the night. Jesus was allowed no defence. He was forcibly struck in the middle of the trial. Later, Pontius Pilate knew the case was a miscarriage of justice, but he allowed Jesus to be crucified anyway. Finally, he was tortured most cruelly.

I wish to describe in detail the place where mercy and justice met – and the amazing name of that place. To the lover of truth it seems that mercy, which is giving what is not deserved and justice, which is giving what is deserved, cannot meet. They are two very different places. How can we get what we do deserve and what we don't deserve at the same time? But in truth, justice, and mercy did truly meet.

In the beginning, when God created the earth, like all builders, he had to establish a foundation. It is the foundation that defines the integrity and the longevity of the building. Herod, the great builder of the Second Temple, understood this: when he built the Temple in the time of Jesus, he built it with stones that weighed in excess of 300 tons each. Thousands of men had to cut them out of the quarry and manoeuvre them by hand into the places where they sit today.

The foundations of the earth and the universe we read of in the psalms were far more massive than the foundations of the Temple we marvel at today. We read that "[God] laid the foundations of the earth" (Psalm 102:25). This is a marvellous thought. God laid the foundations of the earth with a plumb line that had complete integrity. He laid them on the same foundations as the foundations of his throne: "righteousness" and "justice" (Psalm 89:14; 97:2).

When God laid that foundation and created the earth, he brought order out of chaos. It was then, with the foundation of righteousness and justice, that the warring elements were brought together in harmony. When we stand upon the things on which the throne of God is founded, we too begin to see order emerging out of chaos.

Chaos comes as a result of our going our own way, for the sake of power, wealth, prestige, or carnal pleasure. Sin corrupts the integrity of the "walls" of society. It undermines them and places them on shaky ground. History points to so many "fallen walls" that were undermined by men chasing after power, wealth, prestige, or carnal pleasures.

Jesus said of the Pharisees that they were, "full of greed and wickedness... they neglect justice and the love of God" (Luke 11:38–42).

For such crimes he called them "sons of hell" (Matthew 23:15). They had strayed so far from his foundation that they were no longer attached to it. They could no longer be building blocks in his kingdom because they were from "hell" and had a different master and a different foundation. Just as oil and water cannot mix, so those whose hearts were so different from the self-sacrificing, righteous heart of Jesus could not come together with his. They had become incompatible, like two magnets of repelling polarities that will never snap together because of the powerful force holding them apart.

The Temple would be destroyed not many years after Jesus died. Even though Herod built the Temple on such massive foundations, those foundations did not incorporate the ingredients of justice and righteousness.

Justice and the sins of injustice can never be reconciled where truth exists. The self-absorbed man seeking after his own power, wealth, prestige, and carnal pleasure will always undermine the walls of justice and righteousness.

When love and truth came down to dwell among us in the person of Jesus, miracles began to take place. As love and truth indwell us today, miracles take place too.

Now I return to the scene at the beginning of this book – a story of injustice and the abuse of power, but also of the miracle that took place within me, through God's love.

Out there, in the darkness of the lonely veldt, we were victims of a government run by "sons of hell". They were ordering violence, getting their minions to do terrible things to innocent people for the sake of unfettered, absolute power – all so that they could do as they pleased; so that justice would never catch up with them.

The Romans 13:4 function of government, where a ruler is "God's servant, an agent of wrath to bring punishment on the wrongdoer" was being turned upside down out there in the torture camp. The ruler yet again was directing his wrath not at wrongdoers, but the innocent.

Rulers who order innocent people to be tortured or harmed in some way forfeit their right to be called God's servants. They are no longer honouring what a ruler is ordained to do. Rulers who choose to reject Jesus, trample God's law, and persecute their people automatically become servants of the evil one. They become "sons of hell" because nothing evil can come from God.

When my mother-in-law was ordered by the thugs to sing a "Chimurenga" song she was unable to do so because she didn't know any. This was a crime in the brainwashed minds of those loyal party youth.

"Sing any song!" she was commanded. The first song that came into her head was a nursery rhyme that must, I suppose, have been subconsciously buried after singing it to our children. In the chaos of that dark night, with the guns, the bullets, and the beatings, it was farcical in the extreme to have a grey-haired grandmother sing such a song to sixty or more half-crazed, drugged up youths – young enough to be her grandchildren. Her arm was shattered. Mike and I were both in life-threatening conditions with many broken bones and severe bruising. Nevertheless, she was forced to launch into her song, *The Teddy Bear's Picnic*:

> *If you go out in the woods today, you're sure of a*
> *big surprise.*
> *If you go out in the woods today, you better go*
> *in disguise!*

Then came the chorus for all these young boys, who had mostly been forced from their homes, away from their schools and their parents to take part in the ZANU-PF militia and beat innocent people at the torture camps:

> *Picnic time for teddy bears,*
> *The little teddy bears are having a lovely time today!*
> *Watch them, catch them unawares*
> *And see them picnic on their holiday.*
> *See them gaily dance about!*
> *They love to play and shout!*
> *And never have any cares.*
> *At 6 o'clock their Mummies and Daddies will take them*
> *home to bed,*
> *Because they're tired little teddy bears!*

I am not sure if Angela got to the second verse. I don't think they appreciated the irony either. The second verse went:

> *If you go out in the woods today, you'd better not*
> *go alone.*
> *It's lovely out in the woods today, but safer to stay*
> *at home.*[1]

One of them took a burning stick from the fire and deliberately thrust it into Angela's mouth. This horrible act cemented within me the knowledge of the evil to which these men had given themselves over.

I told this story to a person in Cape Town. I said that these people were high on drugs and they were not in their right minds. She scorned my story. "I was a heroin addict for eight years," she confided, "and there was never a time that I did not know what I was doing. That is never an excuse!" she said emphatically.

Mike was groaning but was mostly unconscious. They had wanted him to sign a bit of paper to say that we would withdraw our case from the SADC Tribunal and thereby discontinue our stand for justice. His right hand was broken hideously, with his middle finger sticking out at a right angle. His whole head was swollen and distorted from the severe beating he had received. His left ear looked like a piece of butchered, bloody meat. He was barely recognizable.

I was not in a good state either. I didn't know it then, but my skull had a fracture along most of the left side. My whole head was intensely painful. My right eye was completely closed, and I could not open it. The blows from the rifle butts and the kicks had broken some of my ribs. All I knew was that I had to get away from that evil place. When I was lying face down in the dirt I desperately picked away as well as I could at the knots binding my hands. It was nylon ski rope and the knots were difficult to loosen. Gradually, I could feel a little bit of movement and eventually I managed to get them undone. I started to unpick the rope that was tying up my feet. The difficulty was in concealing what I was doing. I knew that once I was free all I had to do was sprint to the nearest bit of thick bush. If I could sprint the first thirty metres or so it would be difficult for them to catch me. It was very dark and the bush was dense. They were drugged up as well. I figured that I could do it.

Then I thought of what they would do to Mike and Angela if I got away. They were bound to kill them in retribution if I escaped. I decided I had to stay with them come what may and pray. I was resigned to dying. I was completely unafraid of death, though. God gave me complete freedom from fear. I had already prayed that if God wanted me now, I was ready. If he still had work for me down here, then I was also ready.

The young men eventually discovered that I had untied myself and so tied me up very tightly after that. The ropes bit into my wrists and ankles very painfully. I soon lost all feeling in my hands where the blood was cut off.

They decided I needed another beating. Some of them picked me up by my belt and started beating the soles of my feet with a *sjambok* (leather whip). I convulsed with each blow as the pain shot through my body. The torturers were using both arms and all their strength to strike my feet. With each convulsion, my ribs and back hurt terribly. I can remember crying out at each crack, "Jesus!" And then the next, "Jesus!" And the next, "Jesus!"

Angela was worried that neither Mike nor I would survive, even if we were rescued. She prayed that God would at least save my life, for the sake of Laura and the children. There was desperation in her prayer. "Where is God in all this?" she wondered. "Why is he allowing all this?" She was beginning to feel abandoned and forsaken by him. Then she felt God saying to her, "Look up!"

Angela looked up. The African sky on a crystal clear winter night in the middle of the bush is a sight to behold. Hundreds of thousands of beautiful jewel-like stars were set in their constellations – all exactly in their places. There was no chaos up there. Every star was in its place obeying all the natural laws of science that God had designed at the very beginning of time. As she looked up and saw this wonderful array of beauty and order shining down upon us, a sudden peace came over her. She had full assurance that even among the cries of pain, the brokenness, the blood, and the chaos of the evil around us, God was in control. He would be glorified.

When they stopped beating my feet and I was able to slump down on the dirt, I was breathing hard. Each breath was painful because of my broken ribs. I continued to pray. Then the miracle happened.

All through the previous eight years, as soon as the government thugs had started doing terrible things to people I knew – friends, acquaintances, fellow Christians, people I had heard of – I had struggled with the conundrum of how to love these enemies who were bringing such havoc on innocent people.

When preaching the Sermon on the Mount, Jesus told us to love our enemies. But how could we do this? How could we physically muster love in our hearts for people who were doing terrible things to our countrymen and women; who were mutilating God's law? How could we find love for people who were undermining the very foundations of justice and righteousness on which God's throne stands? How, when they were causing mass starvation and suffering in the land, could they be loved?

The answer was simple. They couldn't be loved. Jesus might be able to love them, but I certainly couldn't. I knew it was right to love them, but that didn't make it physically possible to do so!

I had seen too much. So many farmers had come through my office when I was a regional executive officer for the Commercial Farmers' Union (CFU). They were hardened men who had been through war, drought, pestilence, and international sanctions during the bush war of the mid-1960s and '70s – and struggled bravely on through it all. Some of them had bought their farms as young men and carved them from virgin bush, living in mud huts at the beginning and then, as they became productive and established, gradually building proper houses for themselves and their workers. I had huge empathy for these men and their wives. I admired their tenacity and courage; their ability to farm in such hard conditions. I could not bear to see them now, near the end of their lives after a lifetime of toil, at the end of the line with nowhere to go, tears rolling down their cheeks as they asked me what they should do.

How could I find love in my heart for people who had just marched onto their farms, for which they had spent their lives paying, had killed their cattle to roast on dangerous fires set in the farmers' gardens, and had eaten them with the drums beating all night long, threatening death to those who had resisted.

Furthermore, they had been assisted by the police who had refused to act because the authorities had ordered them not to. Even now as I lay in the dust, they were eating the beef they had stolen from Mount Carmel that afternoon.

I remembered being alerted to the murder of another commercial farmer, Terry Ford, early one morning in March 2002. I found him lying in the mud in his own blood, outside his homestead near the fence. He had been savagely beaten and then shot through the head because the president's sister, Sabina Mugabe, wanted his farm. His little Jack Russell, Squeak, who went everywhere faithfully with him, was positioned, cuddled up to him, guarding his body, refusing to allow anyone near him when the police with their black boots and AK-47s finally arrived later that morning. They had refused to come and assist Terry when he'd phoned them during the night in terrible distress. Then that morning they had refused to arrest the perpetrators. Squeak was not going to entrust his butchered master to these people!

Yet Jesus' command to "love our enemies" stands. He tells us to love the people that do these things or order them to be done.

What did Jesus mean? Is it possible to love murderers? Is it possible to love those who steal our homes and livelihoods, leaving a population hungry, suffering, and poor? Is it possible to love those who destroy a lifetime of work; to love those who kill innocent animals as they did on Mount Carmel – over 500 beautiful giraffe, zebra, sable, waterbuck, impala, and other animals that Mike and Angela had brought in and loved and protected? Is it possible when the acts of wickedness continue for day after day, month after month, and year after year to find love for those who kill, steal, and destroy everything we hold dear?

As I lay in that desperate darkness with my bloody wounds, bruises, and broken bones, something amazing happened. Those words, spoken nearly 2,000 years before by the only Son of God, who gave his life for me, came echoing through the centuries and hit my heart as though they were almost something physical:

> *Love your enemies and pray for those who persecute*
> *you, that you may be sons of your Father in heaven.*
> (Matthew 5:44–45)

> *Love your enemies, do good to those who hate you, bless*
> *those who curse you, pray for those who ill-treat you.*
> (Luke 6:27–28)

How could this be? I didn't know how this could be, because it is contrary to human nature. We would be dreaming if we thought it was. It would not be honest. It violates all reason, logic, justice, and good sense.

But there it was. The Living Word had appeared, almost as a physical manifestation in my heart, and it had a remarkable, transforming effect on my whole being. Suddenly I felt an overwhelming, godly love for these people who were doing such terrible things to us. Suddenly, I saw each of them as a person who needed to know that they were loved – loved so much that the only Son of God was prepared to die for them.

I didn't think about what I did next; it was something completely spontaneous. I reached out from the ground where I lay to the nearest pair of legs, with their bare, dirty feet near to my head, and with my tied-up hands touched the legs and said, "May the Lord Jesus bless you!" Then I reached out to the next pair of legs and said the same thing, touching them: "May the Lord Jesus bless you." Then I did the same thing to the next pair of legs. I saw each of these people as a lost soul, needing the transforming love of the One who threw the stars into space. Most were young boys, malleable to the forces of evil, being used by those forces to retain the power they held.

Was this justice that I did such a thing? Of course not! They did not deserve to be blessed. They had done everything to deserve the exact opposite. But that is where the miracle is.

When Jesus came up against the authorities he did not hold back in speaking truth to them. He emphasized truth, righteousness, and justice, in all that he did. He came against everything that impeded truth, righteousness, and justice from breaking through. He wanted the life breathed back into a dying world. He was there to save life, to not allow it to be strangled out of existence by wickedness. On the Sabbath, when Jesus saw a man with a shrivelled hand, he didn't wait until the next day to heal him. He provoked the unjust leaders of his day to their faces and asked the man with the shrivelled hand to get up in front of everyone. Then Jesus spoke directly to the authorities: "Which is lawful on the Sabbath: to do good or to do evil, to save life or to destroy it?" (Luke 6:9). Contained in this brief sentence was Jesus' whole mission – and ours as Christians.

Not only did Jesus "do good" by healing the man with the shrivelled hand, he also "did good" by confronting, to their faces, those doing evil through their hypocrisy, arrogance, greed, and rejection of the Son of God and his ways. That is what upholding justice is all about. In a sense, that is what Mike had done when he challenged the government's acquisition of Mount Carmel farm in the regional court of the SADC Tribunal, confronting Mugabe's ruthless, violent, and systematic destruction of life and property in Zimbabwe.

Here, in the synagogue, at the beginning of his ministry, Jesus was doing good by both confronting the authorities and helping the needy at the same time. The authorities, of course, "were furious". They eventually arrested, tried, and sentenced him, not for "doing evil" and "destroying life", but for being the most perfect man.

When Jesus was arrested and went through his series of unjust trials, he did not call on power from heaven to strike the authorities dead as he could have done. In fact, when he was arrested in the darkness of Gethsemane, he healed the soldier whose ear had been struck off by Peter with his sword. He did not evade the authorities as he could have done. He offered no defence at his trial. He did not raise his supporters up.

Jesus' love for mankind was too great. He wanted to see us saved from the hypocrisy, pride, greed, selfishness, lust, and all the other sins that prevent us from being free. He knew he had to stand as the perfect sacrifice in the place of all who were bound by sin and stubborn hearts. He knew that it was only through him, the truth, that the way could be made open. Justice dictated that this was the only way, because the absolutes of justice and righteousness on which the throne of God are founded cannot be changed. Each one of us would be found guilty, but there is a place where we can stand shielded from the merciless truth of the scorching sun of justice. The cooling shadow is cast by him who made the supreme and perfect sacrifice for us on the cross. He died just as much for the Pharisees who were so furious at him for defying their authority, as the man with the shrivelled hand.

Jesus allowed himself to be made a sacrifice for the men who were beating him – and people throughout Zimbabwe – just as much as he did for Mike, Angela, and me who were being beaten at this moment. He committed this supreme act of sacrifice to bless them, just as much as he did it to bless us. He bled, suffered, and died because he loved them just as much as he loved us.

It is the truth of this supernatural love that is able to stand in atonement for the laws of justice and righteousness and take the punishment that justice prescribes. That is the blessing that Jesus made possible. That is the blessing with which I was able to touch those young boys, out of the supernatural overflow of love that God gave me when I was lying beaten and bleeding in the darkness.

When I touched them and blessed them in the name of Jesus it was as though the ropes that were cutting off the blood supply to my hands and feet were loosed – just like they were "loosed" for the three in the furnace when the "fourth man" appeared.

That night the bonds were broken supernaturally by the inpouring of the love of the Saviour into my heart. His love cleansed and drove out the natural feelings I had towards the people who were persisting in doing such wicked things in the land. The destructive force of bitterness was banished from my heart – and remains so. Suddenly, even though I was still tied up and I was Mugabe's captive, shivering on the ground, I knew I was free. I knew too that the boys in their Mugabe T-shirts all around me could also share in the same freedom.

Shortly after that, we were bundled into the back of Mike's vehicle. I did not know where we were being taken, nor did I have any fear of their plans. One of the leaders had said, "Dead bodies don't speak." In all likelihood, we were being taken away to be shot and dumped into a shallow grave, like so many others during the past few months, but I was not afraid of that. They could not take away the knowledge that I was loved unconditionally by the living God, who promises not to allow us to endure more than we can bear.

Some time later the car stopped. We were carried out. They laid us down on the dirt road behind the vehicle next to two churches.

They undid our bonds, explaining where we were. One of them apologized for what they had done. Then they roared off in their stolen vehicle, through the police roadblock a few hundred metres down the road.

I saw a light and stumbled through a hedge towards it. The house was occupied by frightened MDC supporters. They lent me a phone and God gave me the clarity of mind to remember Laura's number and speak to her coherently. We were free! God had things left for us to do.

That night I experienced and understood what the place where justice and mercy meet is called. It was there, in all its amazing glory, perfectly positioned between justice and mercy in the "cooling shadow" of the Almighty. The place was called grace! Amazing, indescribable, undeserving, unconditional, all-loving, all encompassing grace! There in the shadow of Jesus and his cross lies grace, big enough for all to shelter underneath. Big enough for Peter who denied him; big enough for the Roman soldiers who mocked him and spat upon him, tortured him and crucified him; big enough for Paul who persecuted and killed his followers; big enough for the Pharisees and teachers of the law who had the most perfect man and the only Son of God unjustly killed; big enough for the thugs who had beaten us and who were ultimately the cause of Mike's death; big enough for tyrant kings and rulers if they would only repent; big enough for me!

Jesus told the parable of the Good Samaritan. "What must I do to inherit eternal life?" came the question from the expert in the law.

"Love the Lord your God with all your heart and with all your soul and with all your strength and with all your mind and love your neighbour as yourself" was the answer, for it summed up the entire law.

"Do this and you will live," Jesus said (Luke 10:28).

"Who is my neighbour?" the expert in the law then asked. "And what does it mean to love our neighbour?" we might add.

It is us who have been like the man beaten up on the road, lying there, half dead though often we do not know it. Jesus came for us and travelled the same road. At the cost of his own life he saved us from death. This is the costly grace he bestowed upon us.

Now that we are alive, we must be like Jesus in the story. The despised half-breed Samaritan man was prepared to demonstrate God's grace and demonstrate costly grace.

He didn't hurry past on his way because he was afraid of being attacked himself. He knew he was at an ambush site. The Jerusalem to Jericho road is a winding, mountainous route with plenty of places for thugs to hide out. He knew that if he didn't hurry on, the same fate could befall him. The prudent course of action would have been to get out of there, like the priest and the lawyer who had passed before him. He didn't do so. He was prepared to risk his own life for the life of a stranger.

He was like Bruce, my brother-in-law, who was prepared to risk the bullets of armed men from a notorious youth militia base to try to save us. Jesus wants us to do likewise.

He was like Dirk Visagie and Dana Nel who courageously came out to try to help us that night when we were in the torture camp. The police in Chegutu, Selous, and Kadoma all refused to come out, but they were prepared to risk their lives, unarmed, to try to rescue us. Fortunately, we were set free just before they arrived, and Laura was able to phone them minutes before they would have gone into the torture camp. That was God's timing. Their willingness to risk their lives was a demonstration of costly grace. Jesus wants that willingness from us.

He was like Gift Konjana when he went courageously into another torture camp at two in the morning posing as a ZANU chief with a Mugabe T-shirt and ordered the militia to put the tortured people accused of being opposition supporters into his car. He literally snatched them from the jaws of death, risking his own life in a demonstration of supreme and costly grace. Jesus watches from heaven and says, "Yes, these are the risk takers who will advance my kingdom."

Jesus wants us to take risks for those who need our help.

The Samaritan also showed a willingness to sacrifice. He didn't allow his business plans to get in the way of sorting out a situation that he knew was desperate. Unlike the priest and the lawyer, he sacrificed his former plans, his time, and his money. He was open to an inner compulsion of conscience to show compassion to the poor, beaten stranger lying by the side of the road. He bandaged his wounds and he had his donkey carry him to an inn where he looked after him and paid for professional assistance to bring the man who was "half dead" back to life.

Lastly, he showed a willingness to overcome prejudice. The beaten man was simply someone who needed to be saved. Jesus made him, a despised, hated half-caste, the hero of his story to challenge us to overcome our xenophobic prejudices against people of different backgrounds and races. Jesus did not discriminate. He died for the most wicked, despised outcasts among us. He came to bestow costly grace upon us all. When we experience and understand that grace, we are spurred on to act, to not leave the victims of tyranny bleeding in the dust.

As the church and as individuals we are called to love and change the morally bankrupt world around us, challenging injustice and unrighteousness as we do so. It is only by demonstrating Jesus in acts of justice, mercy and righteousness that this becomes possible.

Jesus said:

> *"For I was hungry and you gave me something to eat,*
> *I was thirsty and you gave me something to drink, I*
> *was a stranger and you invited me in, I needed clothes*
> *and you clothed me, I was sick and you looked after me,*
> *I was in prison and you came to visit me." Then the*

righteous will answer him, "Lord when did we see you hungry and feed you, or thirsty and give you something to drink? And when did we see you a stranger and invite you in, or needing clothes and clothe you? When did we see you sick or in prison and go to visit you?" The King will reply, "I tell you the truth, whatever you did for one of the least of these brothers of mine, you did for me."
(Matthew 25:35–40)

7

PULLING THE CHRISTIAN THREAD THROUGH HISTORY

Abraham Kuyper was a Christian minister and the prime minister of the Netherlands at the turn of the twentieth century. Kuyper, as a church and political leader, reflected on church, State, business, and other associations. He came to the conclusion that the church's mission was to evangelize and nurture believers, in order to send people into the world to influence it in politics, business, art, science, education, and in the media. In Kuyper's view, the church exists to transform and support individuals who, in turn, transform society. He differentiated between the institutional church and the organic church. The institutional church reaches out to communities, to support and guide individuals. The organic church, made of specialist individuals, reaches out to influence the world. The institutional church may also have those who follow specialist paths to speak truth to power. The rest of the institutional church needs to support such people.

Through history there have been such individual Christians who have led the way, pulling the thread of Christianity on, bringing countries out of darkness by raising the standard of truth.

Britain rapidly descended into anarchy after the restraining influence of the Roman legions was withdrawn in AD 410. Historian G. M. Trevelyan says it was a "fearsome chaos of warring tribes and kingdoms, while inside each of these loose political units, family carried on the blood feud against family".[1] Warring barbarian bands of Picts, Celts, and Scots left chaos in their wake. From over the sea came the Angles, or English, invading from today's southern Denmark and the Saxons, invading from today's Germany. The Romano–British civilization, through which Christianity had been introduced in the third century, was crushed and with it the crafts, sciences, and learning of Rome. Towns were sacked and villas deserted and laid waste.

In the insecurity that followed there were two dramatic developments. The first was the resurgence of Christianity. Augustine and his forty or so missionaries were sent from Pope Gregory in Rome to the Anglo-Saxon barbarians. The King of Anglo-Saxon Kent, Æthelberht, was already married to a Christian by the name of Berthe, and Christianity rooted itself quickly. Augustine of Canterbury wrote to tell the Pope that there were already 10,000 people who had been baptized by the next year. King Æthelberht also became a Christian.

Over the next few centuries Christianity became ensconced in the hearts and social fabric of the people. By the time of the Norman Conquest in 1066 the parish system had been developed with parish churches throughout the land and a system of land ownership, law, shire court, and kings.

The other significant development was the grouping together of people in feudal societies. This was a natural progression from the insecurity in the land after the fall of the Romano–British civilization. The people had to protect themselves and they discovered, like the herds on the African plains, that there was safety in numbers. The feudal system was a direct response to insecurity and fear. The feudal State came into being when King Alfred eventually melded the various kingdoms within fragmented feudal England under one head.

Under this system, in order for a baron to pay his taxes and become wealthy and powerful enough to fulfil his obligations to the king, and at the same to protect himself from other "war-lords", he needed the common people to help him – and the common people needed him.

In times of intense insecurity, anarchy becomes a greater threat than despotism. Living on a farm in Zimbabwe we experienced both anarchy – albeit controlled anarchy – and despotism. This evil mixture prevented us, the white commercial farmers – who are considered by Mugabe as "enemies of the State" – from being able to come together to protect ourselves. In fact, it prevented us from being able to protect ourselves at all.

Under the feudal State, people could come under a baron's protection and be bonded to him. Thus they became serfs – bonded to work for the noble, but afforded peace to build their houses and farms on plots of land. During those feudal days the king was above the law and his subjects were not afforded any protection except on his whim. There was nothing that stood between the peasant and the tyranny of the feudal lord or king except, most crucially, the church. Only the church could shield men from the ever-present threat of tyranny. But though the church was of God, like all things that consist of men, it too could be prone to times of abuse of power.

The realm lurched along, dependent to a large extent on the disposition of the all-powerful king. Henry II was a far-sighted and energetic king in the latter half of the twelfth century. He developed a judicial and administrative system and engendered a culture of obedience to government that prevented the recurrence of anarchy. He introduced the famous bench of royal judges that travelled the land, teaching the doctrines of the common law and enforcing it. It was this common law – based upon a mixture of common precedent and common sense, but predicated on the Scriptures – that established the foundation for the future.

With the king's peace under the common law Henry II destroyed over 1,000 unlicensed castles and, unlike the situation in Europe, he made it illegal to raise private armies and fight private wars.

The interest of the English knight changed focus. Instead of having to fight wars, he developed the interests of the country gentleman farmer: improving crop yields, breeding better breeds and bloodlines of cattle and sheep, and generally improving the efficiency of agriculture. Civilization and the path to liberty were suppressing the ages of barbarism and equality was beginning to be blazed.

As agriculture developed under the prevailing peace, the merchant communities and the middle class sprang into being. Manufacturing, trade, and overseas commerce began in earnest.

Historian G. M. Trevelyan reports:

> *Britain began, before any other European state, to develop a nationhood based on peculiar characteristics, laws and institutions… their courts evolved a single system of native law for the whole realm… Common law was a development peculiar to England; and Parliament in alliance with the common law, gave [England] a political life of [its] own in strong contrast to the later development of Latin civilization.*[2]

"Common law," he continues, is the "great inheritance of the English speaking nations."

After the next king, Henry's son, Richard the Lionheart, died, his infamous brother John became king in 1199. King John was a cruel and hated man. He had already proven himself to be treacherous and mean-spirited under Richard's rule. Now as king, John's unreasonable demands of his barons and the people under them was a step too far. It is no wonder that the tales of Robin Hood at that time made a hero out of a villain. Robin Hood and his merry band lived as fugitives in the forest, robbing the rich and giving to the poor. This was also the period of a great Christian awakening taking place among the poor as the Franciscan Movement rapidly spread throughout Europe and beyond (reaching Britain in the 1220s).

More heroic than Robin Hood, but much less well known, were the men who began to constitutionally resist the unreasonable demands of the king. There was a gradual awakening among them to the realization that the institution of law was something with a life of its own, distinct from the power of the king. It was "above him", and he too must be forced to come under its governance.

The Archbishop of Canterbury under King Richard had been a remarkable man, enforcing the king's peace and bringing the merchant classes and knights into running local affairs through the process of election while Richard was at the Crusades. Now his successor, Archbishop Stephen Langton, came to the fore. Langton demarcated the Bible into the chapters we use today. Before him there were no reference points in the Bible except in the names of the books themselves.

Archbishop Stephen Langton was the real, unsung hero of that time. What he did was of such lasting significance that his name should be far better known than Robin Hood!

Perhaps though, he was the ultimate Robin Hood. Amid the tumultuous tussles of the times it was Langton who took the lead in bringing the king to account. In a meadow on a summer's day by the Thames at Runnymede in the year 1215, King John was forced by those under him to bow to the law. He rode onto the field proudly and arrogantly above the law; he walked off it the very same day with head bowed low, beneath the law. He had signed what came to be known as the Magna Carta Libertas – the Great Charter of Liberties.

Archbishop Langton was the genius and the moral strength behind this act of huge and lasting significance. He had robbed the king of his absolute power and given it to the people. Sovereignty had been taken from the king and given to the community of England.

The Magna Carta was limited, but it was practical. Therein lay its brilliance. It opened the door for the movement that eventually created liberties for all. In the Magna Carta, the king's will was no longer arbitrary. Now there existed the right to due process in law. No freeman could be punished except through the law. At Runnymede a bridle bit had been inserted into the king's mouth. He no longer had free rein to exploit and ravage wherever he willed.

Lord Denning, arguably the most influential English judge of the twentieth century described the Magna Carta as "the greatest constitutional document of all times – the foundation of the freedom of the individual against the arbitrary authority of the despot".[3] It was the first great step towards equality before the law. It led the way in the "Model Parliament" shortly afterwards, where the king had to acknowledge that there could be "no taxation without representation" – the cry that was to lead to American independence five centuries later. It assigned practical remedies to temporary evils and would fire the imagination of those fighting for freedom under law for centuries to come. It was the door that opened the way to the parliamentary system developed in England and that has since been adopted around the world.

Though the safeguards given in the Magna Carta did not directly protect the serf, the community of serfs would, through a chain effect, become indirectly protected from both anarchy and tyranny. The golden door was open to the road that would lead to liberty under law becoming a reality through the Glorious Revolution and beyond. That road was still a long one though, and it is good to acknowledge some of the great milestones along the way, where Christians played their part in being salt and light in the nation.

A century later, the Yorkshireman, John Wycliffe (1328–84) was born. He came into the world at a time when there was latent corruption and immorality within much of the church. The pharisaical sale of indulgences was rife at that time: people were paying priests to be free from their sins and there was increasing worldliness among the bishops and clergy.

Wycliffe preached that the indulgences the clergy were selling were a fraudulent deception and a criminal act of simony. As a prominent Oxford scholar and churchman he was instrumental in stopping England paying taxes to the Pope as, "Christ alone is the Head of the church." He went further, advocating that the church needed to develop a Christlike attitude to its great wealth and vast properties (which covered about a third of the land of England) and that they should be forfeited.

In his book, *Civil Dominion,* he maintained that the ungodly and wicked had no right to rule because their ungodliness and wickedness became the modus operandi with which they ruled. This was not what God had ordained government for. Wycliffe's bold and outspoken adherence to the truth would profoundly influence history.

He became convinced that many in the church had strayed away from the truth. He had a deep and fervent belief that the Scriptures were the authoritative centre of the Christian faith and that all truth was found in them. He believed, like the German monk and Catholic priest, Martin Luther (1483–1546) more than a century after him, in justification by faith alone.

His most enduring enterprise was his fervent desire to make the truth available to the common man without the mediation of priests. He realized that the common man needed to be able to read and understand the Scriptures for himself if he were to find and be absorbed in the freedom of the truth. He would later be known as "the morning star of the Reformation".

John Wycliffe went on painstakingly to translate, with various others, the whole Bible into the English language – a job he finished in 1384, the same year he died. It was the first complete European translation of the Bible since it was translated into Latin 1,000 years before. Suddenly the common man had direct access to the truth in the word of God. It was the spark that would later set alight the hearts of the people of Europe with the Reformation.

Wycliffe's inspirational work soon influenced Jan Hus (1369–1415), a Czech reformer in Bohemia. Hus was particularly inspired by Wycliffe's teaching. The truth, Wycliffe had taught, was central to the whole Christian faith. Still today, the Czech motto is a quote from Hus: "Truth conquers".

Much later, Hus became a great hero of Václav Havel (1936–2001), who led the movement that threw off the communist yoke in Czechoslovakia. "For hundreds of years," Havel said, "the name of the master Jan Hus has been inscribed in the mind of the nation, especially for his deep love of the truth."[4] Today the Czech Republic celebrates a Jan Hus holiday each year.

The band of Christians inspired by the teaching of Hus came to be known as the Moravians. These committed Christians sent missionaries throughout the world. It was the Moravians that were instrumental in the transformation of another great hero of the faith, John Wesley of England, a prime mover in the Great Awakening.

Hus was branded a heretic and later burnt at the stake, where Wycliffe's manuscripts were used to fuel the fire. At his death Hus prophesied, "My goose is cooked ["hus" means "goose" in Bohemian] but a hundred years from now a swan will arise whose voice you will not be able to silence."

A hundred and two years later in 1517, Luther was to nail his ninety-five theses against indulgences to the church door in Wittenberg and fan the flame of Christian revival and reformation that would burn throughout Europe and then across the globe into the present age.

Professor Montagu Burrows, a historian at Oxford University, wrote about the influence that Wycliffe had on history:

> *To Wycliffe we owe, more than to any one person who can be mentioned, our English language, our English Bible, and our reformed religion... in Wycliffe we have the acknowledged Father of English prose, the first translator of the whole Bible into the language of the English people, the first disseminator of the Bible amongst all classes, the foremost intellect of his times*

brought to bear upon the religious questions of the
day, the patient and courageous writer of innumerable
tracts and books, not for one, but for all classes of
society, the sagacious originator of that whole system of
ecclesiastical reformation…[5]

After Wycliffe's death he too was declared a heretic and his body was exhumed and burnt on the orders of Pope Martin V. The truth cannot be burnt, however. Today the Wycliffe Bible Translators have managed to translate the Bible into over 850 different languages all over the world.

Great things were starting to happen in England. Due to Archbishop Langton and the far-reaching effects of Runnymede, freedom and peace had further encouraged the early stages of the agricultural revolution which began around 1540. With the wool that was produced a cottage industry developed. Individual initiatives among people from all classes involved spinning wool, dyeing it, and weaving the beautiful cloths that England became known for. The English wool trade was the basis on which the merchant classes built their business and plied it all over the known world. It was the basis on which the Tudor and Stuart navies came to rule the seas and explore and trade throughout the new world. In the centuries to come, the lands and peoples of those far-off lands would be the "mission fields" to which many missionaries would give their lives.

The great cathedrals, the universities of Oxford and Cambridge, the representative assemblies, were built. "Public" schools such as Eton were established. The emancipation of the serfs took place, towns grew, English literature began to blossom, and Caxton's printing press began to replace the monastic scribe. Voyages of discovery and exploration were made. The plays of Shakespeare were written.

Peculiar to England, the Renaissance took on a very Christian slant with ancient Greek and Hebrew being learned and the Bible being brought alive by Oxford reformers such as Dean Colet. Colet also built the prototype of the reformed grammar school at the dawn of the sixteenth century, opening the door for more and more people to be able to study the truth in the Scriptures.

The Reformed Calvinist Puritans were persecuted by Charles I and many fled. A mighty tussle had begun as King Charles tried to spit out the bridle bit of Runnymede. In 1629 the king dissolved Parliament, which was made up of many Puritans, for the fourth time in those first four years of his reign. In that year the young king began his period of "personal rule", referred to by the Whigs in Parliament as "the eleven years of tyranny". King Charles believed in "the divine right of kings". He did not need Parliament to rule with him. He believed, like King John, that he was above the law and accountable to no one above his person.

Due to his persecution, from 1630 to 1640, more than 20,000 Puritans went to carve out a different life in the new American colony of Massachusetts. They took with them their Puritan Protestant faith, which became the centre of their society. Their aim was to reform their new world and conform it to God's law. As such, they had a more profound influence on American law and society than anyone else throughout America's history. It is, I believe, largely by building on this foundation that America was able to become so successful – from those humble beginnings, it grew to be the superpower of the world it is today.

The Puritans who remained in England joined the Parliamentary forces and civil war began against the tyranny of King Charles. With their general, Oliver Cromwell, they fought to usurp the divine right of kings. When their forces prevailed, Charles, at his trial, defended himself with the maxim that "the king can do no wrong". He was finally publicly beheaded in 1649 after his trial in London, and the republican Commonwealth under Cromwell was formed.

In the crisis that resulted from Cromwell's death, Charles's son was summoned back from exile and restored to the throne as

Charles II in 1660. The English constitutional monarchy had been resurrected, but the Puritan Parliament was eager to ensure that the king did not overreach himself in the climate of absolute monarchy and unbridled power that prevailed in Europe at the time.

In the same year that Charles II was crowned king, a cousin of his, Frederick III, the king of Norway and Denmark, established what was known as the King's Law. It was solemnized in 1665 and stated that the monarch "shall be revered and considered the most perfect and supreme person on the earth by all his subjects standing above all human laws and having no judge above his person". The dangers of such extravagant power were abundantly evident to the Puritans of England.

Charles II had his hands full with at least a dozen named mistresses and many illegitimate children. He initially let Parliament have its way. In 1670, however, he signed the secret Treaty of Dover with another cousin, the French king, Louis XIV – the "Sun King" – another who believed in the divine right of kings and who is famously credited with having said, "L'état, c'est moi!" ("the State is me!"). This infamous treaty would involve Charles receiving two million crowns for publicly converting to Catholicism. He also committed to assisting the French in fighting the Protestant Dutch.

Charles II, like his cousins, also believed in "the divine right of kings". Indeed, in 1683 he beheaded Algernon Sidney for declaring in *Discourses Concerning Government* that the right to rule was vested in the people. John Locke fled to Holland before the same fate overtook him.

Charles died before more harm could be done, and his younger brother James, the last of the Catholic kings, succeeded him in 1685. James II was a womanizer like his brother, but more ambitious in his desire to become an absolute monarch like his Sun King cousin across the channel, now at the height of his power. James II prorogued Parliament within seven months of ascending to the throne and so ruled alone for the rest of his reign.

He said famously, in the arrogance of great dictatorial tradition, that "Kings are not bound to give an account of their actions."

He appointed Catholics, who constituted perhaps 2 per cent of the entire population of England, to high office throughout the land and had a law made that people found to be attending illegal, refractory Presbyterian meetings would be "punished with death and confiscation of property". Within a year he had dismissed many of the judges that he felt he could not manipulate to do his will.

To add further injury, the following year he arrested the Archbishop of Canterbury and seven of his bishops on charges of seditious libel, for not reading out James's declaration of indulgences – a step towards re-establishing Catholicism in England. In an act of civil disobedience the Archbishop of Canterbury, William Sancroft, had refused to read out the king's declaration, knowing that if he did, it would eventually lead to the persecution of the people. Rather, he and six other bishops exercised their right of petition, preserved in the Magna Carta. They delivered this to the king on 18 May 1688, just prior to having read it out. On 8 June, at the decision of the Archbishop of Canterbury, the bishops refused to obey the court summons, and King James arrested them and put them in the Tower of London to await trial. The ire of the people of England was up. It looked like civil war would again tear the land apart.

Shortly after, when James had a son, destined to be brought up a Catholic prince, the Protestant population of England took decisive action. Within three weeks, a group of seven nobles sent Rear Admiral Arthur Herbert on a secret mission disguised as a common sailor.

Among the "immortal seven" was the Bishop of London, Henry Compton. He had already had a run-in with the king when, in a deliberate act of disobedience, he refused to obey the king's orders to ban the king's chaplain, John Sharp, from preaching. The king suspended John Sharp anyway and removed Bishop Henry from his post as Bishop of London.

Bishop Henry knew Princess Mary, the king's daughter, having been her tutor and having officiated at her wedding to King William of Holland.

Rear Admiral Herbert sailed across the North Sea clutching an important letter to King William in The Hague. The letter invited William (who was also James's sister's son) to take the throne of England with Mary. It read in part:

> *the people are so generally dissatisfied with the present conduct of the Government, in relation to their religion, liberties and properties (all which have been greatly invaded), and they are in such expectation of their prospects being daily worse, that your Highness may be assured, there are nineteen parts of twenty of the people throughout the kingdom, who are desirous of a change; and who, we believe, would willingly contribute to it, if they had such a protection to countenance their rising, as would secure them from being destroyed.*[6]

William started making preparations. He was especially worried after the French had concluded a naval agreement earlier in the year with James II, and he knew that if James and Louis XIV formed a closer alliance, as seemed likely, he would not be able to withstand a joint attack by the English and French. William's preparation was complicated by the fact that it was getting late in the season and winter was not a time when wars were fought.

Fortunately the French forces became involved in Germany. He knew the time was right. By the October, in an amazing feat of organization, he had assembled his force at Hellevoetsluis. He set out with 463 ships, 40,000 men, 5,000 horses, his artillery, supplies, and everything required for a fully fledged invasion. Significantly, for the Protestants and the defenders of the Reformation, the year was 1688. It was exactly 100 years after Sir Francis Drake and the Royal Navy had defeated the Spanish Armada in 1588.

Their first attempt at invasion was foiled by a north-westerly gale. Undeterred, William reassembled and resupplied before sailing again on 1 November from Hellevoetsluis, relying mostly on wind and circumstance to dictate where and when they should land.

The wind took him south and then west, and it was only on 5 November that William emerged from thick fog and landed at Torbay in Devon after eluding the Royal Navy. It was the anniversary of the gunpowder plot, when Guy Fawkes and Catholic conspirators had attempted to blow up Parliament and the Protestant king, James I, in 1605. To commemorate "Guy Fawkes night", many had taken to burning effigies on bonfires after James II had converted to Catholicism. So when William landed on the shores of England on 5 November 1688, it was on the tidal wave of an auspicious moment. The Glorious Revolution was about to take place.

On 9 November, William rode into Exeter on a white horse, surrounded by a most incongruous sight for those times: 200 black men from the Dutch colonies in America, dressed in regal white robes. As William and his well-disciplined army marched towards London, there was little or no resistance from the supportive English population. On 24 November, James II's key general, John Churchill, deserted him. Two days later James's younger daughter, Princess Anne, did the same. Throughout the next few weeks the people rose in anti-Catholic uprisings around the country in the places where King James had promoted Catholics to high office.

On 9 December, King William's advance guard of 250 men fought King James's advance guard of 600 Irish Catholic troops. The people of Reading fired on King James's men, and King James's troops fell back in disarray with the loss of a few dozen men. That was the only battle in the entire revolution.

Realizing that he had no support from his people, his army, or even his own family, King James fled, throwing the royal seal that was used to recall Parliament into the Thames as he went. He was recaptured trying to make his way to France but, not wishing

James to become a martyr, William allowed him to escape just before Christmas.

The House of Commons and the House of Lords agreed that James had abdicated and that the throne had been left vacant. After agreement on a "Bill of Rights" that would protect the people of the kingdom from future tyranny, William and Mary were asked to become joint king and queen.

On 11 April 1689, William and Mary were crowned by Bishop Henry Compton.

The Glorious Revolution of 1688 was a defining moment in the history of the world. Absolute monarchy had been overthrown by an established constitutional monarchy. The Bill of Rights that underpinned it was heavily influenced by John Locke who travelled back from exile in Holland to England with Mary, the future queen. Locke was a friend of Isaac Newton and the Earl of Shaftsbury, under whom he had written *Two Treatises of Government* in 1679 – a document that was only published in 1689. It was a work influenced by Locke's Puritan and Calvinist upbringing and background. He advocated strongly the separation of powers in government and stated that revolution was not only a right, but an obligation in certain circumstances. His greatest legacy remains his influence in the development of property rights both in Britain, then America and throughout the world. Property, he argued, precedes government.

The American Bill of Rights and the American Constitution a century later copied verbatim some of his writings. Every other bill of rights ever written since that time has been influenced by Locke. Thomas Jefferson, the principal author of the American Declaration of Independence in 1776 and twice President of America wrote that Locke, Bacon, and Newton were his trinity of "the three greatest men that have ever lived without exception".

The Christian-inspired Enlightenment that drove the Glorious Revolution powered onwards. Before the Glorious Revolution there had had been no formal banking system. The Catholics had prohibited it on the grounds that to charge interest was usury. John Calvin made the revolutionary argument that paying rent for a house or a horse was no different than paying rent for the use of someone else's money, so it was permissible for a financier to charge interest. The banks in Calvin's Switzerland were the net result.

In King William's Protestant Holland, Amsterdam had become the financial capital of the world. William had borrowed money from the financiers of Protestant Amsterdam to part fund the Glorious Revolution. Now in England, the Bank of England was established within five years and many other banks were formed thereafter. The foundation was laid for London to take over as the financial capital of global commerce soon afterwards. People could now save money and earn interest on that money and entrepreneurs could get finance for great developments.

With the new peace and the protection of property rights through the law, the agricultural revolution took off. The Leicester sheep and the shorthorn cattle were bred. Leguminous fodder crops such as clover increased nitrogen levels in the soil and made cropping sustainable. Turnips were also brought in as a major crop, reducing the amount of fallow land. The fens and other wet areas were drained. Britain became the most efficient agricultural nation in the world with only 22 per cent of its workforce in agriculture by as early as 1850 – able to feed a population that had grown from just over 5 million at the time of the Glorious Revolution to 17 million within just over a century. The workforce was thus freed up for the Industrial Revolution to take place.

The transport revolution also began, with Britain's first new public roads being built since the time of the Romans. With cotton and other commodities in America finding markets in a more prosperous Britain, and the surplus commodities from the agricultural revolution needing transport to markets, a new transportation network was required to move these commodities. The "turnpike roads" were built through private enterprise, the finance generated through the new banking system. By the 1830s,

30,000 miles of roads had been built. At the same time, private enterprise built the canals, yard by yard, by hand. The considerable capital was secured against title for privately owned land. Within just over a century of the Glorious Revolution there would be approximately 3,000 miles of canals criss-crossing the country.

The individual suddenly mattered. He and his property were now fully protected by law and his private endeavours could be justly rewarded. People were becoming wealthier on a sustained basis for the first time in history. Britain led the way as the vanguard of the movement for free trade.

Great inventions took place and were patented in Britain, since the patent laws protected the property rights of the individuals who had made these inventions. Within a short period, 80 per cent of the world's cotton textiles were being produced in Britain to be exported throughout the world. In the early 1800s Britain started to develop the world's first railway network.

What people do not ponder very often is how the environment had been created to allow the agricultural, financial, transport, and industrial revolutions to take place with the incredible developments, inventions, and sustainable wealth they created. Why was it that Britain led the way? The roots are clearly entrenched in the philosophy of the Glorious Revolution and the Enlightenment. It was the people's firm belief in God and his truth for individual lives, coupled with the individual's responsibility towards ensuring government was there to facilitate the protection of the individual and his property that led the way. These God-fearing people were prepared to overcome the fear of man and stand for the truth, come hell or high water.

Despotic systems of government, where power is concentrated in one person, always lead to times of unpredictability and insecurity. Individuals don't count and their God-given potential for good is suppressed by an oppressive system. Under "personal rule", peace becomes a fragile luxury. As the old saying goes, power corrupts and absolute power corrupts absolutely. Under dictatorships and in the absence of peace where injustices are able to flourish, it is the people who suffer, because poverty and misery are the net result.

Economic historians all agree that the Industrial Revolution was a pivotal event in the history of humanity. It took place with the recognition of the truth of two godly principles: the protection of the individual and his property, and the freedom of the individual under godly law.

Craig Richardson, an Associate Professor of Economics at Winston-Salem State University (USA), has written brilliantly on property rights and their foundational importance for economic growth, as well as for the alleviation of poverty through the property titles bringing capital to life. He describes property rights as being analogous to the concrete foundation of a building: critical for supporting the frame and the roof, yet virtually invisible to its inhabitants.

Richardson says there are three distinct economic pillars that rest on the foundation of secure property rights, creating a largely hidden substructure for the entire marketplace:

- Trust on the part of individuals/investors that their investments are safe from potential expropriation;
- Land equity, which allows wealth in property to be transformed into other assets; and
- Incentives, which vastly improve economic productivity, both in the short and long term, by allowing individuals to fully capture the fruit of their labours.

Despotic systems of government are reinventing themselves in the current age and will cause the people to stumble as we move into the age to come. There is a grave danger of larger governments with their ever-larger bureaucracies mutating into huge, unwieldy feudal systems, which are impervious to granting continued autonomy and freedom to the independent individual. As Christians we need to be concerned that we are getting ever closer to the scenarios described in Revelation. We must stand in the truth by preparing ourselves for that time.

8

RISING FAITH, TURNING TYRANNY: SPARKS OF HOPE

The word "tyranny" comes from the Greek word *turannos*, which meant "king" or "unconstitutional ruler" to the democratic Greek states. Tyranny is the rule of men, rather than the rule of a higher law that cannot be changed. The Greeks recognized that human authority had to be limited if that authority was not to be taken advantage of and abused.

In Zimbabwe we have adapted to living under tyranny. There are many who have not thought much about what the correct Christian response to it should be.

There was a clear understanding in the early church that the law was something from God to preserve justice. Indeed, St Augustine of Hippo, acknowledged as one of the greatest Christian thinkers of all time, wrote that "an unjust law is a contradiction in terms".[1]

When unjust laws are made or when State-sponsored murder, rape, theft, and other wicked things take place, we need to work out how, as Christians, we should respond.

There are many in the modern age who consider Christianity to be a pacifist and apolitical religion, which teaches that getting involved with the wider injustices within nations is incompatible with God's teaching. In the early church, when Christians were still very much in the minority, there was not an awful lot they could do within the nation as a whole. There was no critical mass to make much difference in the affairs of the Roman Empire. God led Paul to Rome, to the political hub, just as Joseph had been at the hub of the Egyptian Empire and Daniel at the hub of the Babylonian Empire. Satan was desperate to thwart him from getting there.

Again and again, I have heard the argument in Zimbabwe that Christians should not go to the hub and speak out. Getting involved in speaking against injustices that emanate from the hub is "political". Prayer marches are considered to be "political". Court cases to defend those who have had injustices committed against them by people in the ruling party are considered to be "political". Anything, in fact, that might stop the tyrant having his way is deemed "political". Thus, the belief that the church should not have anything to do with politics becomes an excuse for cowardice, weakness, and a blinkered "hear no evil; see no evil; speak about no evil" approach. Adolf Hitler is reputed to have once said, "What luck for the rulers that men do not think."

During the rise of faith in the Reformation, John Calvin wrestled with the issues of unjust government and what to do about it. Writing about magistrates, who had much more power than they do today, he said that they were "appointed to restrain the tyranny of kings" and "officially to oppose the undue license of kings".

Calvin also wrote:

> *But in that obedience which we hold to be due to*
> *the commands of rulers, we must always make the*
> *exception, nay, must be particularly careful that it*
> *is not incompatible with obedience to Him to whose*
> *will the wishes of all kings should be subject, to whose*
> *decrees their commands must yield, to whose majesty*
> *their sceptres must bow. And, indeed, how preposterous*
> *were it, in pleasing men, to incur the offence of Him for*
> *whose sake you obey men! The Lord, therefore, is King of*
> *Kings. When He opens his sacred mouth, He alone is to*
> *be heard, instead of all and above all. We are subject to*
> *the men who rule over us, but subject only in the Lord.*
> *If they command anything against Him let us not pay*

*the least regard to it, nor be moved by all the dignity
which they possess as magistrates – a dignity to which
no injury is done when it is subordinated to the special
and truly supreme power of God.*[2]

The passage so often quoted to justify inaction against tyrants is
Romans 13.

*Everyone must submit himself to the governing
authorities, for there is no authority except which
God has established. The authorities that exist have
been established by God. Consequently, he who rebels
against the authority is rebelling against what God has
instituted, and those who do so will bring judgment on
themselves. For rulers hold no terror for those who do
right, but for those who do wrong. Do you want to be
free from fear of the one in authority? Then do what
is right and he will commend you. For he is God's
servant to do you good. But if you do wrong, be afraid,
for he does not bear the sword for nothing. He is God's
servant, an agent of wrath to bring punishment on the
wrongdoer. Therefore, it is necessary to submit to the
authorities, not only because of possible punishment but
also because of conscience.* (Romans 13:1–5)

Paul's letter to the church in Rome was written shortly before his
journey to Rome and subsequent imprisonment, where he would
eventually be beheaded by the Roman authorities under Nero nine
years later.

In Peter's letter, written in Rome four years before he was
martyred in the same year as Paul, he says:

*Submit yourselves for the Lord's sake to every authority
instituted among men: whether to the king, as the*

> *supreme authority, or to governors, who are sent by him*
> *to punish those who do wrong and to commend those*
> *who do right… Show proper respect to everyone: Love*
> *the brotherhood of believers, fear God, honour the king.*
> (1 Peter 2:13–17)

The problem comes when the king and the authorities, far from "punishing those who do wrong", reward them; and far from "commending those who do right", condemn them.

It was on this Romans 13 subject that Revd Jonathan Mayhew, a 29-year-old Boston minister with four generations of missionary descendants among the Indians preceding him, preached a sermon on the centenary of the beheading of Charles I. It was entitled, "A Discourse concerning unlimited submission and non-resistance to Higher Powers". He concluded that,

> *upon a careful review of the apostle's reasoning in*
> *this passage, it appears that his arguments to enforce*
> *submission, are of such a nature, as to conclude only*
> *in favour of submission to such rulers as he himself*
> *describes; i.e., such as rule for the good of society, which*
> *is the only end of their institution. Common tyrants,*
> *and public oppressors, are not entitled to obedience from*
> *their subjects, by virtue of any thing here laid down by*
> *the inspired apostle.*
>
> *I now add, farther, that the apostle's argument is so*
> *far from proving it to be the duty of people to obey, and*
> *submit to, such rulers as act in contradiction to the*
> *public good, and so to the design of their office, that it*
> *proves the direct contrary. For, please to observe, that if*
> *the end of all civil Government, be the good of society;*
> *if this be the thing that is aimed at in constituting civil*
> *rulers; and if the motive and argument for submission*
> *to Government, be taken from the apparent usefulness*

> of civil authority; it follows, that when no such good
> end can be answered by submission, there remains no
> argument or motive to enforce it; if instead of this good
> end's being brought about by submission, a contrary
> end is brought about, and the ruin and misery of society
> effected by it, here is a plain and positive reason against
> submission in all such cases, should they ever happen.
> And therefore, in such cases, a regard to the public
> welfare, ought to make us withhold from our rulers,
> that obedience and subjection which it would, otherwise,
> be our duty to render to them. If it be our duty, for
> example, to obey our king, merely for this reason,
> that he rules for the public welfare, (which is the only
> argument the apostle makes use of) it follows, by a
> parity of reason, that when he turns tyrant, and makes
> his subjects his prey to devour and to destroy, instead
> of his charge to defend and cherish, we are bound to
> throw off our allegiance to him, and to resist; and that
> according to the tenor of the apostle's argument in this
> passage. Not to discontinue our allegiance, in this case,
> would be to join with the sovereign in promoting the
> slavery and misery of that society, the welfare of which,
> we ourselves, as well as our sovereign, are indispensably
> obliged to secure and promote, as far as in us lies.[3]

This Boston sermon, preached in 1750, came to be known as, "the morning gun of the revolution". Everyone read it. From it the motto of the American Revolution, "resistance to tyrants is obedience to God" was coined.

Emmanuel Mounier stated that, "It is not force that makes revolutions, it is light."[4] This was the beacon of light for the independence movement of America.

The theologian, Francis A. Schaeffer, recognized as one of the most influential Christian leaders of the twentieth century wrote,

the State is to be an agent of justice to restrain evil
by punishing the wrong doer, and to protect the good
in society. When it does the reverse it has no proper
authority. It is then a usurped authority and as such it
becomes lawless and is tyranny.[5]

In his *Christian Manifesto*, he challenged Christians that, "If there is no final place for civil disobedience then the government has been made autonomous, and as such, it has been put in the place of the living God."

"At a certain point," he says, "it's not only the privilege but it is the duty of a Christian to disobey the Government."

In Maoist China, Stalinist Russia, Hitler's Germany, or Mugabe's Zimbabwe, truth demands that we confront unjust laws and unjust governments. If we do not, we start to become irrelevant in the wider society in which we live. The unique freedoms of Western Europe and the English-speaking world are a direct result of Christians making their voices heard and their actions felt in the societies in which they lived. The foundation of law, based on the godly revelation of truth in the Scriptures, is not arbitrary. It is deeply and world-changingly spiritual. God's kingdom has to advance with his law and not without it.

The English theologian John Stott wrote:

If the State commands what God forbids, or forbids
what God commands, then our plain Christian duty
is to resist, not to submit, to disobey the State in order
to obey God… Whenever laws are enacted which
contradict God's law, civil disobedience becomes a
Christian duty.[6]

"We should not ask, 'what is wrong with the world?'" he said, "for that diagnosis has already been given. Rather we should ask, 'what happened to the salt and the light?'"[7]

The trouble is, as Christians in the twenty-first century, we are allowing ourselves to be conditioned to simply tolerate the intolerable and accept the unacceptable, because we feel impotent to push against the world system. But, according to Steve Camp:

> *Tolerance is not a spiritual gift; it is the distinguishing mark of postmodernism; and sadly, it has permeated the very fiber of Christianity. Why is it that those who have no biblical convictions or theology to govern and direct their actions are tolerated and the standard or truth of God's Word rightly divided and applied is dismissed as extreme opinion or legalism?[8]*

While we cannot tolerate a situation where intolerance crushes love, we cannot allow a tolerance that compels the truth to flee. This precarious walk of intolerance to evil, in an attitude of love, requires godly wisdom. We require the fire of love and truth to burn bright in our breasts if we are to move along the path set before us as the church in the twenty-first century.

The Israelites came to a point before the sacking of the Temple and the exile when, "[the priests] dress the wound of my people as though it were not serious. 'Peace, peace' they say when there is no peace" (Jeremiah 8:11). Tolerance of all things in the name of peace is not godly. The pursuit of peace paralyses lasting progress in the establishment of the Kingdom of God if it is at the expense of the truth and the pursuit of justice.

John Stott says, "The incentive to peace-making is love, but it degenerates into appeasement whenever justice is ignored. To forgive and to ask for forgiveness are both costly exercises. All authentic Christian peace-making exhibits the love and justice – and so the pain of the cross."[9]

Zimbabwe has seen a great rise in faith over the years, but at the time of writing, tyranny still reigns. Gonçalo da Silveira was the first missionary to visit the land. He arrived at the royal court of the Munhumutapa (master pillager) in the north of Zimbabwe the day after Christmas in 1560. The Arab traders intrigued against him and, seventy days after arriving, he was strangled on the king's orders and thrown to the crocodiles. Although at least a dozen more Jesuit missionaries arrived over the next century, no more Christian activity took place after 1667.

A century and a half later, Robert Moffat came onto the scene. He was a product of the Great Awakening that took place in Britain and America. Men like Wesley, born shortly after the Glorious Revolution and founder of the Methodist and holiness movements, which led to the Pentecostal and charismatic movements, had done much to stir people up to become missionaries. Seeking justice and righteousness and sharing Christ and his saving grace throughout the world became their mission.

Christians like William Wilberforce, motivated by a desire to put Christian principles into action to serve God in public life, were already active. He led the way as a Christian reformer, pushing Christian values and social responsibility into the public sphere. He was intent on reviving Christian moral values in the land.

Wilberforce was approached by the Quaker anti-slavery committee. At that time an estimated three people out of every four around the entire world were slaves. No "civilization" in the whole of human history had existed without slavery. Through a lengthy campaign that involved research on slavery, pioneering lobby work, letter writing, debating, getting parliamentary petitions signed, and writing pamphlets and books, he introduced the slavery abolition bill, which was eventually passed in 1807, a decade before the young Moffat got to Africa. Finally in 1833, three days before he died, the slavery abolition act was passed to cover the whole British Empire, which would lead the way for the rest of the world to do the same.

Meanwhile, Moffat trekked to Kuruman for the first time in 1818, a little oasis on the edge of the Kalahari Desert with a flowing spring known as "The Eye". Two years later, at the age of twenty-five, he and his wife with their soon to be born daughter Mary, were in the great African interior, building the famous mission station which would be their base for the next fifty years – the "fountain for Christianity" in southern Africa.

The Moffats were there for a whole generation before the Afrikaner "Great Trek" from the Cape. They were a lone, little white family in the middle of the veldt, hundreds of miles by ox wagon from any help in those turbulent and treacherous days. Though it was more than 300 years since Europeans had first landed in southern Africa, the interior was still very wild. Among the native tribes clothes were unknown, the wheel had not been conceived, written language was unheard of, and there were no calendars – each day simply merged into the next. There was no law apart from the word of the chief, and life was a struggling, precarious affair, weaving its way through times of anarchy and total tyranny.

When the Moffats got to Kuruman, the Zulu leader Shaka was reaching the height of his bloody reign in Zululand to the east. Mzilikazi, one of Shaka's most brilliant generals, was forced to flee after he failed to hand over all the looted cattle from one of his plundering raids among the Sotho people to the north. He set up his royal kraal in the then Transvaal, a few miles north of modern-day Pretoria. His system of government was along the same lines as Shaka. He became an absolute monarch, ruthless and feared by his own people and by others throughout the land. He had large regiments of young men at his beck and call that would plunder the tribes around, leaving only death and tears in their trail.

When some of Mzilikazi's men came to spy out the mission the Moffats had developed, Moffat offered to protect them by escorting them back to their king, an 800-kilometre or so round trip in an ox wagon. They traversed some of the devastated wasteland where hundreds of thousands of people had been killed – perhaps more than a million – in the previous decade or so, first by Shaka and then by Mzilikazi.

Moffat describes the "melancholy devastations" that he passed through during the months of his first trek to the king and of the "numerous ruined towns through which we daily passed [which] were once very populous". It was "a land that mourned" Moffat wrote in his journal.[10]

Moffat witnessed tyranny in an absolute form at the royal kraal. "His word is law... everyone seemed to tremble before him... all know that his frown is death."

Moffat writes that, "no one dare utter a single word of disrespect either of the king or his government. Such a remark would be followed by almost instant death... I had never before known such relentless cruelty."[11]

Nobody owned anything apart from the king. Only he could decide who could slaughter cattle and who would receive what meat. The young men needed permission to marry or sleep with the virgins of the tribe – and sometimes this was denied for years. The king's many daughters from his reported 400 or so wives were not allowed to marry at all – and if they had sex with a man they would be killed. "All the people as well as what they possess are considered Moselekatses [Mzilikazi's]." On a later visit, he wrote, "His people are a nation of slaves. Everything animate or inanimate is his."[12]

Moffat recorded that an approach to the king had to be done by crawling in a subservient, cowering way, addressing him by several of his many "praise names": "Tau e tuna" (great lion), "ntlou enkholu" (great elephant), "Tla Mantota" (the man slayer), "Molimo" (god), "Nkose a makosi" (King of kings), etc.

> *From childhood to youth their minds are imbued with fear of him... he, Moselekatse, knows, and some of his people know, that where the gospel has been received, there is liberty of speech and liberty of action, and that wherever it prevails it will oppose tyranny and despotism...*[13]

The missionary and the tyrant king struck up a strange and touching friendship, which would last over three decades. The king looked up to the simple missionary of truth as an honest and trusted father figure who had much to teach him. Over the years, Moffat was the only man who could speak forthrightly to the king of the wrongness of his ways without being killed.

Moffat did much to try to enlighten the king, and the king did much to temper his excesses of tyranny over the decades that Moffat visited him, first in the Transvaal and later across the Limpopo. Sadly, he never became a Christian. It would have meant a complete change in his life and system of government, which relied on total fear for control, and his plundering raids for provisions. He would no longer be the centre of everything in his kingdom if he allowed people out from under his spell of fear and gave them liberty to speak truth and to own property. Although in 1859 Moffat was finally able to set up the Inyathi Mission in Matabeland, years before any other white men settled between the Limpopo and the Zambezi, they did not have freedom to preach and nobody was allowed to become a Christian.

What Moffat did achieve over the Limpopo was to sow the seeds for Christian mission and transformation. The next mission station was set up by the Jesuits in 1880. Although Lobengula, Mzilikazi's son, did not allow any more missions, when the pioneer column arrived in 1890, mission stations were set up across the country with approximately fifteen mission farms started in the 1890s. John Baur, who wrote *2000 Years of Christianity in Africa*, says this was "a record number in early mission history".

Back at Kuruman, Moffat learned the Setswana language and translated the entire Bible as well as *Pilgrim's Progress* into Setswana himself, over a 29-year period. He set up his own printing press so that he could personally print Bibles for the people. He built a school and taught the people to read and write at a time when there was no written language in the African interior. He built irrigation canals and experimented agriculturally, teaching the people modern agricultural systems. By 1834 he already had 500 acres that could be irrigated. He set up a forge and a blacksmith's shop to make agricultural implements. He organized the people against warring raids in the midst of the turmoil of despotism and genocide to the east and earned abiding respect.

Khama III of the Ngwato people of Buchuanaland, now Botswana, was born when Moffat had already been at Kuruman for a number of years. By then Moffat had brought the young Dr David Livingstone to be with him. Khama's father, Sekgoma (or Sekomi) was convicted that he needed to change. He pleaded of Livingstone, "I wish you would change my heart. Give me medicine to change it for it is proud, proud and angry, angry always."[14]

Three years later, the young Dr Livingstone married Mary, Robert Moffat's daughter. They left Kuruman and went to live with Chief Sechele, whom Livingstone taught to read. The young Khama learned to read as well, and the seeds for his conversion to a life-changing knowledge of Jesus Christ were sown as he read the Bible that Moffat had translated and printed. Other German missionaries, under Heinrich Schulenburg from Natal, also spent a couple of years in the region, and Khama was baptized with his brother in 1862. Khama was transformed as a believer in the truth. One of Moffat's fellow Scottish missionaries from Kuruman, John Mackenzie, was sent to Chief Sechele, chief of the Kwena people of Bechuanaland, and Khama was mentored into true discipleship by him for over a decade.

After becoming a Christian, Khama married a Christian girl called Bessie. When he refused to take any more wives and follow other tribal customs, his father tried to assassinate him. When this failed, a second assassination attempt was made, but his father was then forced to flee. His uncle, whom Moffat had rescued from Mzilikazi, then took the reins as the chief of the Bamangwato and he too made an attempt on Khama's life.

In obedience to the command to honour his parents, Khama invited his father back to lead the tribe. Unfortunately, things did not work out yet again and war broke out.

Khama faced a dilemma. Did God command a pacifist stance in all situations? Augustine of Hippo had pondered how to handle the invasions of the Roman Empire by the savage tribes from the east in the third century, and he coined the phrase "just war". Khama decided that as a last resort a war had to be fought. He was an able leader, and within a month the war ended with him as victor.

He was duly installed as the Nkosi (king) in 1875 and radically revolutionized his people's government. He followed the truth, bringing in sweeping reforms that honoured God, protected life, promoted liberty, and instituted the development of private property. He abolished the Bogwara ceremony at the end of the training of the regiments of young men, where one of their number was sacrificed to appease the spirits. He then made the youths do community service, building schools and churches. He brought in ploughs and wagons and other agricultural equipment and started modernizing the country. He banned the import of alcohol into the country. He made polygamous marriages illegal. He brought in a law that his people must observe the Sabbath day. He allowed private ownership of property and even entitled daughters to be able to inherit from their parents. He went as far as to abolish the payment of tribute by vassal tribes under him.

When threatened with occupation by Germans, Boers, and Matabele, he negotiated that his country should become a British protectorate. Later, when Cecil Rhodes, through the Chartered Company, wanted to colonize Bechuanaland, he travelled all the way to London to personally request the protection of Queen Victoria in 1895. Though Rhodes was powerful, Khama was much fêted by the people of England, who knew of his great efforts to build a sober and godly nation. The great white queen was anxious to meet him. Khama succeeded in persuading Queen Victoria to keep his country as a protectorate. Before he left the palace, she presented him with a beautiful Bible in which she inscribed the words, "The secret of Khama's greatness".

The early missionary journeys of Moffat and Livingstone would move like a ponderous tortoises across the landscape. Each day they succeeded in traversing perhaps ten miles, but as the days wore on, the persistence, courage, and tremendous tenacity of those early travellers was rewarded first with hundreds and then thousands of miles of land being traversed. Slowly, imperceptibly at first when compared to the rapid pace of development in the rest of colonial Africa, the people of Bechuanaland moved forward as a result of the new faith and the new ways of thought and freedom that their faith brought with it.

Khama's grandson, Seretse Khama was born in 1921, two years before Khama III died. Seretse went to Oxford University and while at the Inner Temple, studying to be a barrister, he married Ruth, a white Englishwoman. This caused a terrible hullabaloo in both national and international circles. Black people and white people could not possibly marry. Remarkably, after a series of meetings with the tribal leaders and his people, they accepted that a white woman could be married to their paramount chief. The British, under the Labour government, were not so amenable. Due to pressure from the apartheid government in South Africa, which had recently banned all mixed race marriages, the British banished Seretse from his own country in 1951 and asked the Bechuana people to find a new chief. They refused to do this, and it was only when Seretse Khama abdicated as paramount chief that he was able to go home with his wife and young son, Ian, who was born in exile. When independence came ten years later he went on to lead his country as their democratically elected leader in 1966 – a post he held until he died in 1980.

The British did little to develop the Bechuanaland infrastructure, although its institutions, based on the British system, were sound. Being a landlocked country, with most of its area consisting of the waterless Kalahari Desert, it did not have an awful lot going for it. At the time of independence, Botswana was the third poorest country in the world.

President Sir Seretse Khama was known for his integrity and adherence to truth wherever he went, and this was passed on to those around him. He made sure that corruption remained almost entirely non-existent in his country. Regular multi-party democracy was established with credible elections held regularly. A cosmopolitan non-racial attitude to whites was engendered, and the Christian principle of all being equal before the law was upheld. Liberalized trade policies were adopted. Low and stable taxes were put in place to encourage foreign investment and not penalize successful business. Individual property rights were established and protected. Government was kept small, and in the first decade it was decided that no army would even be established. Rather, a defence treaty was signed with Britain in case of an international threat. Good economic and other advisors were strategically sought internationally and employed. National debts were kept to a minimum. IMF and World Bank loans were avoided. A free society was instituted.

Before the diamond mines were producing wealth, Botswana had already become the fastest growing economy in the world. When diamonds were found, they were managed responsibly and the money has been used to build the infrastructure of the country and benefit the people. Where diamonds are a curse in so many other countries, in Botswana they were a blessing. Perhaps the worst thing that could have happened in Zimbabwe was the recent discovery of the Marange diamonds, reported to be the biggest diamond field ever discovered, currently being looted by ZANU-PF and their Chinese allies with horrifying human rights abuses having been perpetrated against the local people and informal miners, particularly by the military.

Under Sir Seretse Khama, Botswana stood out as a unique example of enduring, corruption-free, good governance to all of Africa.

After Sir Seretse died, the legacy lived on. Botswana's leaders remained honest, responsible, and prudent and their country continued to move forward. In 2008, Ian Khama, Khama III's great grandson, was elected leader. Corruption, defined by Transparency International as "the abuse of entrusted power for private gain" continued to be negligible. Botswana was listed by Transparency International as the least corrupt nation in Africa in 2012 by a huge margin – coming at number 30 out of 176 countries globally.

Good, honest, just leadership – a legacy of the Christian principles actively chosen by Khama III – has without doubt been the key to Botswana's success. Botswana was the fastest growing economy in the world over a period of over thirty years from independence.[15] From being the third poorest country in the world at independence, Botswana climbed to being the second richest in Africa. Only the tiny state of Equatorial Guinea with its massive oil (and very corrupt government under Obiang, who has ruled for thirty-four years) was "richer". Botswana is now the fifty-eighth richest of 185 countries in the world,[16] while Zimbabwe has dropped to being the second poorest on the same ranking.

There is no doubt for us who look across the border that Botswana remains a shining light demonstrating what can happen when a government sticks to fundamentally honest Christian principles.

Sir Seretse Khama understood both the principles of a democracy and the pillars of political freedom. As the British philosopher and writer, Roger Scruton, explained recently on BBC Radio 4's *A Point of View*[17], democracy alone cannot guarantee personal and political freedom; political freedom depends on a delicate network of institutions:

1. First among them is judicial indepence.
2. Then there is the institution of property rights.
3. Then follows freedom of speech and opinion.
4. Finally, there is legitimate opposition.

Government without opposition is without any correction when things go wrong, Scruton said.

Back in Zimbabwe some sparks of light have flared in the darkness. The brightest of these was an outspoken archbishop who spoke truth to the nation. When I first met Archbishop Pius Ncube, I was struck by his humility. There was no pomp or self-righteous pride about him. He was simply a godly man with a heart for the people. He was born in 1946 in Matabeleland of peasant farming stock near Filibusi. After being educated at church schools, he went on to study philosophy and theology and was ordained as a Catholic priest in 1973. "Catholic schools," Archbishop Pius told the *New York Times*, "taught me to put faith first."[18]

In 1983, three years after independence, Pius's return to Zimbabwe from Rome coincided with the four-year-long Gukurahundi genocide of the Matabele people. As thousands of innocent villagers were brutally murdered, many disappearing without a trace, and others were slaughtered in front of family members and terrified neighbours, Father Pius, then a parish priest, was working at a mission station near Bulawayo. He was drawn into the human rights arena, personally helping Bulawayo's former archbishop to take harrowing statements from witnesses of the atrocities.

In 1998, he was ordained the first black Archbishop of the Bulawayo Diocese. In an interview in 2007 he told the local *Chronicle* newspaper, "I never thought that one day I would lead a 120,000-member Roman Catholic diocese, reporting directly to the Pope."

With the chaos that exploded at the new millennium, the new archbishop got involved. The Amnesty International candle wrapped in barbed wire, a symbol of pain and struggle, featured prominently at a service in June 2002 to mark the UN International Day in Support of Victims of Torture. It was attended by a high-level group of South African church leaders, many of whom had been outspoken critics of the apartheid regime.

Local ministers explained that the church had also been affected by the climate of repression and that Archbishop Ncube had suffered a vilification campaign in response to his bold stand of speaking the truth to power. Methodist and Anglican clergy told how they had been arrested and held for several days for organizing public prayers for peace.

"As church, we need to stand up for our rights in Zimbabwe, whatever the consequences. We are called to travel in the way of the cross," said Revd Noel Scott. He was jailed and went on trial later for being part of a prayer march in the run-up to the 2002 presidential election.

During the service, the South African bishops led a solemn procession of victims of violence and torture, together with members of the congregation, carrying 160 large wooden crosses to the altar. They represented the people who had been killed since 2000 when the land invasions and intimidation of opposition activists had begun.

Men and women came forward to relate testimonies of assault by soldiers, police, and gangs of armed thugs. They had sustained disfiguring cuts and burns and had limbs broken in attacks where weapons such as iron bars had been used. Many reported that their homes had been burnt down and entire villages had been torched. They said that the seeds of hatred and bitterness were being sown in the lives of their children who were suffering dreadfully.

Archbishop Pius warned that their traumatic testimonies were only the tip of the iceberg. He said that food was being distributed selectively to ZANU-PF supporters and that hungry children were not being fed. Staff at clinics were instructed to refuse medical treatment to opposition party members, including young children. He said the country was sick because it had leaders who were sick. "Those who continue with their evil practices will be judged by God," he warned.

The first week of June 2003 had been declared by the opposition MDC to be a week of mass action and a stay-away from work. Accordingly, Harare and Bulawayo and most of the smaller centres had been almost entirely shut down. In response, the government had brought out a formidable force of firepower against the people, assembling the army, the police, and the militia on the streets.

As many as 800 MDC leaders and supporters had been detained, including MDC leader Morgan Tsvangirai and his secretary general, Welshman Ncube. Anxious people stayed in their homes, afraid to risk being beaten or tear-gassed if they were seen on the streets.

On the last day of the stay-away, the people of Bulawayo were called to pray for Zimbabwe at an interdenominational service at the imposing, century-old St Mary's Cathedral. Journalist Maggie Kriel captured the atmosphere of the event:

> *It was a profound moment in my life. A thousand folk of all colours and creeds, all holding hands inside the beautiful St Mary's Cathedral, all reciting the Lord's Prayer in devout unison, when overhead, flying low and aggressively, came the drone of one of the army helicopters.*
>
> *Not one person there even faltered, not one turned his head skywards... Many had been in hiding from the regime's despicable police force and secret police, and yet not one person showed any fear, any surprise, any anger, indeed any single emotion as the helicopter swooped past, not once but twice in blustering arrogance.*
>
> *And then, as the noise faded into the distance, the congregation lifted its voice in the haunting refrain of Nkosi Sikelel iAfrika (God Bless Africa); it was quite the saddest and yet the most beautiful, most haunting refrain I have ever heard...[19]*

Prior to the service the situation had been tense. CIO operatives and senior army officers had arrived at the cathedral and had interviewed Archbishop Pius. He had been instructed not to march after the service, that there was to be no politics in the church, and that no testimonies could be given. This did not stop people from flowing into St Mary's throughout the service until the vast, vaulted nave was full, nor Pius from going ahead with the reading of the lesson from Luke 4:18:

> *The spirit of the Lord is upon me, because he has*
> *anointed me to preach the gospel to the poor. He has sent*
> *me to proclaim release to the captives, and recovery of*
> *sight to the blind, to set free those who are oppressed…*

It also did not stop Archbishop Pius from referring to the country's "evil and satanic regime", nor the congregation from confidently raising their open hands while the army helicopter circled noisily overhead.

Archbishop Pius described the ongoing harassment he faced in a BBC interview: the stalking by Mugabe's intelligence agents, the death threats, the attempted smears on his reputation in the State-controlled media. "I will not allow myself to be muzzled," he vowed.[20] But the harassment was taking its toll. A few weeks earlier he had suffered an attack of Bell's Palsy, a neurological condition often brought on by stress.

The pressure and vilification intensified. Sharon LaFraniere from the *New York Times* reported in 2004 that, "In May, Mr Mugabe called the archbishop 'an unholy man', another Desmond Tutu, whom he dismissed as 'an angry, evil and embittered little bishop.' Last week Mr Mugabe accused Archbishop Ncube of 'satanic betrayal' of Zimbabwe."

Ray Motsi, a Baptist pastor in Bulawayo, told LaFraniere that, like Archbishop Tutu, Pius was a beacon of light. "He is a very brave person, very single-minded. He has been able to discern the moment and understand what is the most important role he can play."[21]

LaFraniere was right when she noted that many churches had been torn apart under President Mugabe, divided among those who backed him, feared him, openly opposed him, or simply did not want to hear about the tyranny that stalked outside the church door.

Archbishop Pius continued to be an inspiration to us though. A report on the Good Friday Procession in 2005 read:

> *The law has been bent, twisted and broken where*
> *necessary, to preserve Mugabe and his cronies in power,*

and a raft of draconian security legislation employed to strike fear into the hearts of any would-be dissenters. That is what marks this Good Friday Procession in Bulawayo as special. The walkers are risking arrest and imprisonment, at the least, for just walking down the street together, bearing crosses, en route to an ecumenical service held in another of the city's churches. Looking around the small crowd who set off from the Cathedral, one is aware that at least half of them have already incurred the wrath of the Mugabe regime and spent a weekend or two – or more – in the city's squalid police cells as a result…

All this morning's walkers are aware of the risks. Indeed it is the omnipresent fear factor which has prevented many others from joining them – and which has made Archbishop Pius Ncube, who leads the procession, such a lonely figure among a national church leadership that has allowed itself, in large measure, to be cowed into silence. The ecumenical group, "Christians Together for Justice and Peace", which is behind this event, provides one of the few more honourable exceptions to a picture of shame.

Remarkably, the police did not intervene on this occasion to stop the procession or to arrest any of those participating. Perhaps it was the element of surprise on the part of the organizers which found the police and their informers unprepared. Perhaps it was the presence of a few election observers, or representatives of the foreign press here to cover the elections, which restrained them. Or, just perhaps, the prayers of the faithful for deliverance from ungodly rule are at last being heard.[22]

As the country spiralled into chaos and fear that threatened to engulf whole communities, ordinary Zimbabweans looked increasingly to Archbishop Pius for leadership and direction – and he did not fail them, speaking out fearlessly against the regime and continuing his vital work among the poor, orphaned children, the elderly, and the homeless.

When Operation Murambatsvina began and the homes of hundreds of thousands of families were demolished during mid-winter without warning, Archbishop Pius castigated the Mugabe government publicly, worked tirelessly to assist the destitute, and co-authored a report on the destruction entitled "Zimbabwe's Tragedy is Africa's Shame".

A year later, on 26 June 2006, with the pressure on his government intensifying and the economy crumbling, President Mugabe spoke at the phony National Day of Prayer he himself had called in response to some of the churches starting to raise their voices. Criticizing Archbishop Pius, he warned, "When church leaders start being political, we regard them as political creatures and we are vicious in that area."

Commenting on the poorly attended event, political chameleon Jonathan Moyo, a former information minister, said that Mugabe had long wanted to involve the churches in his political plans and that this effort would continue.[23]

On 11 March 2007 we were shocked when a horde of riot police attacked opposition officials and supporters en route to a prayer meeting organized by church groups in Harare. As photos of beaten and bloodied men and women, including Morgan Tsvangirai, were beamed across the world, international condemnation of the regime mounted.

Mugabe needed to get dissenters out of the way. The church was starting to take its place in the nation, largely through the courageous inspiration of Archbishop Pius. His voice was raised relentlessly against government-sponsored injustice. The CIO and nefarious church infiltrators launched a malicious and very messy smear campaign against the "meddlesome priest" regarding an alleged affair. As fears for his life mounted, Archbishop Pius was recalled to the safety of the Vatican and barred by the Vatican from speaking to the media or making further pronouncements on the government or the ongoing crisis in his country.

Revd Graham Shaw, a Methodist minister who stood shoulder to shoulder with Archbishop Pius on many occasions, wrote that,

> *for Pius Ncube, every human being has an innate, God-given dignity which must always be respected. Any dictator who dares to trample on that spark of divinity will surely face his fury.*
>
> *At a time when any sign of dissent was being ruthlessly suppressed and when most church leaders remained silent, this man of God fearlessly spoke truth to power. He spoke without any calculation of the personal consequences. He called the regime and those who did its bidding to account before the God of truth and justice, and in so doing he touched a raw nerve. In effect he was calling into question the moral and political legitimacy of Mugabe and his party, and this was precisely where he and they were most vulnerable.*[24]

Revd Noel Scott knew Pius long before he became a bishop. He commented:

> *What the spirit of God was saying and directing became a motivating force in Pius's life. He had a vision for a new Zimbabwe where everyone mattered and was free and empowered to fulfil their God-given destiny in a society where there was justice and peace.*[25]

Father Nigel Johnson SJ, Catholic Chaplain at the University of Zimbabwe before moving to Bulawayo, said that even though the regime had stopped the street processions in Bulawayo they hadn't been able to ban church services. Archbishop Pius, anxious to give others courage to speak out against the suffering and evils, did this – not just with words, but more powerfully through symbolic actions. "At one service, representatives each came up to place scores of white crosses around the sanctuary, each cross representing a victim of torture," he recalled.

"Since it was difficult for people to stand up in public and give their testimonies, Pius stood close behind them to give them support and courage. This was a moving experience, and even more dramatic when one woman collapsed in his arms after recounting her own torture experience," he said.[26]

Khethani Sibanda, an MDC activist who suffered horrific torture at the hands of the regime in 2001 and was incarcerated in solitary confinement for eight months before finally escaping to South Africa in 2005, told PBS Frontline in an interview that Archbishop Pius had so inspired him as young man that he too "wanted to be tall like him, brave like him and a man of character like him".

"He is a great, great man. I'd rate him among [people like] Mahatma Gandhi... he meets Mugabe, tells him the truth. The media come to interview him, he tells the truth... he is the conscience of the nation."[27]

Now sixty-six years old, Archbishop Pius lives in western Zimbabwe's Hwange Diocese where he continues his selfless work with the poor and orphaned children and leads a life dedicated to prayer.

"He has always stood for the people and takes his role as a shepherd very seriously," Revd Ray Motsi, president of the Theological College of Zimbabwe said.

Revd Graham Shaw believes that Archbishop Pius's courage had a profound impact on Christian leadership in Zimbabwe. "When he was taken from the Church, tragic though that was, it brought about a broadening of the base of prophetic leadership which hitherto had tended to leave most of the truth-speaking to one man," he said. "Though we in positions of leadership in the Church had failed Pius by withholding our full support, he did not fail us. His example continues to inspire."[28]

Archbishop Pius's impassioned plea rings down the years: "Free the oppressed. That is our calling."

9

THE TRUTH WILL SET YOU FREE!

To really make a difference as Christians in the world, and particularly in places where governments have stumbled, we need to do as the writer of Hebrews encourages us:

> *let us throw off everything that hinders and the sin that*
> *so easily entangles, and let us run with perseverance*
> *the race marked out for us. Let us fix our eyes on Jesus,*
> *the author and perfecter of our faith, who for the joy*
> *set before him endured the cross, scorning its shame,*
> *and sat down at the right hand of the throne of God.*
> *Consider him who endured such opposition from sinful*
> *men, so that you will not grow weary and lose heart.*
> (Hebrews 12:1–3)

The two tools of tyranny are quite simply fear and lies. In throwing off the cloak of fear, we also need to tear down the curtain of lies and deception. This can only be achieved by turning to the truth.

Jesus constantly prefaced his statements with, "I tell you the truth…" More than eighty times in the gospels, he says, "I tell you the truth…" It is his most oft-repeated statement. He needs everyone to know that he is telling us "the truth". Indeed, he revealed to us that he is "the Truth" (John 14:6). When we fix our eyes on him, we fix them on the Truth. Truth was at the absolute core of everything he said and did. He told us that, "the truth will set you free" (John 8:32). He equated "the way" and "the life" with "the truth" as a trinity that rested in himself.

If the "father of lies" (John 8:44) is to be vanquished, we must hoist the truth flag high above everything else in our set of moral values. From the truth, everything else flows. When individuals and societies start to become "economical" with the truth, they make a mistake that becomes very costly.

It was in dark, smoky huts that the majority of feudal Europe made their homes, just as much of Africa does today. Traditionally, these abodes had no windows or chimneys. In the smoky darkness everything is murky. Similarly, windows of light that allow the truth to shine in only appear in society whenever Christ is preached.

The Greek philosopher, Plato, emphasized four cardinal virtues: (1) justice – treating with fairness those we interact with; (2) fortitude or courage in the face of adversity and injustice; (3) prudence – the act of weighing the consequences of our actions before we rush to make choices; (4) temperance, expressed in self-discipline and self-restraint. But all of Plato's virtues, like all other virtues admired in the world today such as wisdom, loyalty, generosity, sympathy, and civility, presuppose the paramount virtue of truth. Without truth, nothing ever adds up correctly. If a God-centred truth is not present, some of these virtues can be used dangerously for evil ends. A courageous and loyal supporter of an evil dictator or an evil law is an immeasurable liability to the people as a whole. Even the most vicious and wayward tyrant can do comparatively little damage without loyal sycophants, whose loyalty to a leader, a cause, or a set of orders becomes more important than the pursuit of the truth.

Symond Fiske, a South African agricultural economist, conducted an interesting survey in South Africa. He asked people to rank Plato's four virtues with the other five virtues outlined above, adding honesty as a tenth. In the ethnic mix it was evident that there were different priorities for different ethnic groups.

In the Bantu cultural mix, "fewer than eight percent… put both honesty and justice among the three qualities they valued most highly in a 'good man'". Among Africans of European origin it was "almost forty [per cent]".[1]

Fiske observes that, "A century ago there were few worse infamies in Europe than making a false statement. In African culture it was… more often excusable… Here incivility and disloyalty were both worse crimes." He laments though that the European value of honesty is being lost because "they are turning their backs on the religion that gave their parents and grandparents the strength to stay honest in the face of temptation and hardship. And their families are falling apart…"[2]

I conducted a similar exercise at a small, ethnically mixed church in Zimbabwe. Twenty-six per cent put both honesty and justice within their most desirable first three – although honesty was among the top three in 73 per cent of cases. It seems that the paramount value of truth needs more teaching.

Albert Schweitzer, the Nobel Peace Prize winner for 1952, who devoted most of his life to being a medical missionary in the Gabon observed that:

> *All over the world the evolution of ethics is such that its first great achievement is the high estimation of truthfulness. Man makes the step forward from lower to higher ethics, not by recognition of kindness to his neighbour but by his condemnation of lying, deceit and perfidy.*[3]

When we accept that the word of God is the truth, and we stand for it, we take the quantum leap forward. The apostle John writes:

> *In the beginning was the Word and the Word was with God and the Word was God. He was with God in the beginning. Through him all things were made; without*

him nothing was made that has been made. In him was
life and that life was the light of men. (John 1:1–4)

As Christians we understand that the Word is the truth; and truth is the author and generator of all light and life. He dwelt among us. Where people adhere only selectively to the truth, the power in it starts to be lost. We must nurse the truth, for in it everything else is held together.

In 1192, James Egremont-Lee and I were the first people to canoe the Rufiji river in Tanzania, all the way to the Indian Ocean. It is a wild river, running through the largest game reserve in Africa. Back then, there was nobody there. For a whole 28-day stretch of canoeing we saw not a soul.

The rains had just begun. With tropical rainstorms, capsizes, and hippo attacks, everything began to get damp, including our matches. We realized that if we were to be able to cook and keep the lions at bay at night, as well as have warmth and light, we would have to carry fire with us in our canoe. We made a fire carrier with a tin and a pot, and every few hours would go into the shore to blow the coals into life and get a new fire going. Through the night and the rainstorms we would nurse the fire and make sure it never went out. Through careful commitment to keeping those coals alive we managed to carry that fire with us for weeks.

Those coals are a metaphor for the truth. The same truth for which Jan Hus was burnt at the stake needs to burn in us. The same truth that motivated Wycliffe to give his life to make the truth available to the common man needs to motivate us. The truth that Khama spoke to his people; that Archbishop Pius spoke to the Zimbabwe leaders; that Archbishop Tutu continues to speak to South African leaders needs to continue to be spoken. The coals of truth inside us need to be nursed, nurtured, fed, and blown into life through each day and night. The truth is like the fires on the Rufiji that allowed us to eat and keep the lions at bay and have warmth and light.

The truth protects and provides. Societies that do not put the truth at the top of their value system have always foundered. A society which does not prize the truth as its most important value is like a ship without an anchor in a gale close to the shore. It will inevitably be smashed up upon the rocks.

In the church, we need a regeneration of the Puritan passion to preach the undiluted truth. The truth is not an optional extra in the bid to progress society and develop nations. The church needs to say it as it is: the truth is the building block on which a government will see its people's security established, its businesses thriving, its hungry fed, its children educated, and its elderly and needy cared for. Christians need to be envisioned with the transforming, liberating power of the truth. If the truth is raised to the highest place in our hearts and minds, the commonwealth of the people will be established.

If the church does not forthrightly confront governments that flaut the truth, who lie and steal and are rotten with corruption and with people who act above the law, it is not fulfilling its Christian mandate.

In a very short time in Zimbabwe the stifling force of corruption has taken root, based on greed and a disregard for the importance of the truth. Many Christians have resigned themselves to having to pay their way in bribes. Business, they say, can't go forward any other way. They thereby reject the truth. The cost of dishonesty eventually causes businesses to fail and with that education, health, roads, water infrastructure, and the country as a whole.

In the Old Testament, prosperity and the well-being of a nation is always linked to righteousness – an extension of the truth. The prophets preached against unrighteousness and untruthfulness to God since it always led to the nation falling.

In the Western world, the greatest influence on popular culture today is the New Age – an "anything goes", hotchpotch belief system based on a little bit of truth, but a great deal more deceptive mysticism and subjective sentiment. The West's development assistance in Africa has proven to be so spectacularly unsuccessful because the absolutes of the truth and justice have received so little attention.

What the NGOs, government agencies, and the whole development world does not grasp is that when the truth (and justice, which stems from it) are diminished in the moral value system, meaningful development will always stall. Trillions of dollars of taxpayers' money from the West will continue to pour into a bottomless pit until truth and justice become sacrosanct. Governments in Africa, and elsewhere, that are only stumbling along and periodically falling flat on their faces with truth and justice obscured from their primary vision – will never lead their people out of poverty and oppression. There needs to be a complete refocusing led by those who know and believe in the truth.

The Marshall Plan[4] philosophy has not worked in Africa because truth has not characterized the majority of predatory, post-independence governments. If governments would only concentrate on protecting their people's lives, ensuring that an honest and efficient justice system made criminals accountable, and provided honest title deeds for people's individual properties, then Africa would leap forward.

In Rhodesia, without any of the billions of dollars of aid money that countries to the north of the Zambezi received, health care was better, education was broader, the infrastructure was more developed, agriculture was more productive, and its industry became the second biggest in sub-Saharan Africa. Food aid had never been heard of. This was primarily because business at that time was essentially honest and hard working.

There are those in the post-Christian West that punt traditional African values as the way forward for Africa, but it is clear that when these values were in place before, they did not support many people or lead to very much progress. The old joke of the Afro-cynics about the definition of democracy for the African nationalist leaders was "one man, one vote, one time". The first three decades of African "independence", up to the late 1980s, saw not a single head of state voted out of office.[5] Only Botswana, Senegal, and the tiny state of The Gambia had any sort of credible elections, with Botswana standing head and shoulders above the rest. The others were not truthful in their practice of "majority rule".

Pre-Christian British values were no different in this regard. It was when pre-Christian British superstitions were actively abandoned and replaced by the truth that gigantic leaps were made in living standards, life expectancy, and general well-being. The value of truth that made Britain, Europe, and America great is tragically not being properly passed on – and Africans are losing out.

Where the truth is not pre-eminent, production costs become inflated because the wastage factor is so much greater. There are huge competitive inefficiencies in having to employ security guards, set up sophisticated security systems, buy insurance, and for the owner of each business to have to spend most of his time checking on unreliable quality controllers or on what scam his workers are up to next. In business as a whole, when too many people cannot be trusted to do what they agreed they were going to do, failed business and poverty is always the net result.

Investors know that Africa is the richest continent on earth in terms of natural resources and agricultural potential, but they hold back from investing because they do not know when their investment or savings might be stolen or destroyed by the government of the host country. To the extent that governments practise or tolerate the antisocial behaviours of stealing, lying, corruption, and nepotism, their people will remain poor and their countries underdeveloped.

We need to champion the transforming power of truth. Two plus two can never equal anything but four. Just as everything in the universe is bound to obey the elegant, beautiful laws God has sewn into its fabric, so we must obey the laws of truth and justice he has set before us, designed to cause us to thrive and flourish as individuals, families, societies, and nations on this earth.

When the stalk of an apple breaks, the apple falls from the tree onto the ground because of the law of gravity. If someone throws the apple upwards as far as he can, it will fight the law of gravity, but soon come back down to earth. When individuals, families, societies, and governments are dishonest and fight the laws of the truth God has ordained, they may seem to succeed for a while, but they will come crashing down. Broken people, families, societies, and countries are the inevitable result.

Every law made by man has to be a formal extension of the laws that God has already given man. When I write to Zimbabwe's legislators about dishonest laws in the new draft constitution, where "discrimination is unfair... unless it is shown to be fair" and do not even receive a reply, I realize that our politicians, even the Christians, are being dishonest to the truth.

The truth brings trust and it develops individual responsibility. In business, transaction costs become negligible where there is truth. They are also very much quicker. Business with dishonest people generally fails. The track record soon gets marred and people do not wish to continue doing business with those who have proved themselves to be dishonest. After first one bank closed on us with all our savings, then a bit later our pension scheme got swallowed up like everyone else's, and then the foreign currency in another bank was also liquidated, our trust in the honesty of the banking system of Zimbabwe naturally disappeared. With the printing of money we were eventually working with 100 trillion dollar notes (a trillion is 1 with 12 zeros after it) – and that was after 25 zeros had already been slashed over a period of two years. Within a few weeks even this note could not buy a loaf of bread – if a loaf of bread could be found. Everyone's savings vanished into the ether while those in power became very rich using official exchange rates to convert Zimbabwe dollars into hard currency.

In countries where dishonesty allows injustice to thrive, hope of a better life among the ordinary people is not able to come to fruition. The magic formula to sustainable development is to make the truth the locomotive that will pull all the rest of the carriages along with it.

When Khama broke the age-old system of African government it was by making the truth and integrity his rallying standard. He made his own power, position, prosperity, and passions subservient to the truth. When he put his own well-being below the well-being of the commonwealth of his people, his country began to flourish.

If governments followed Khama's example of turning to the truth, the current 1 per cent of the world's foreign direct investment that goes into Africa would balloon exponentially. Meaningful investment simply does not take place when the truth is not paramount.

When Samuel was old, his sons took over as the last judges in Israel. Unfortunately, the truth is not simply inherited by one generation from their predecessors. It has to be actively chosen. Samuel's sons were not truthful judges: "They turned aside after dishonest gain and accepted bribes and perverted justice" (1 Samuel 8:3). Quite simply, the government stumbled because truth was not at its heart.

Government is about selecting people of virtue and ability in our communities to settle disputes – to be "the people's representative before God" (Exodus 18:19). Just before God gave the law to Moses at the beginning of Israel's life as a nation, Jethro, Moses' father-in-law, imparted some wisdom regarding how a representative government of judges should be made up:

> Select capable men from all the people – men who fear God, trustworthy men who hate dishonest gain – and appoint them as officials over thousands, hundreds, fifties and tens. Have them serve as judges for the people at all times but have them bring every difficult case to you... (Exodus 18:21–22)

Government representatives should not only subscribe to the truth, they should also "hate dishonest gain".

The dishonesty of Samuel's sons was not something exclusive to them. The people of Israel were being dishonest to the truth when they demanded a king. Rather than blowing the coals of truth to life and instituting God's system of government, they let the coals go cold. Samuel warned them of what would happen:

> *This is what the king who will reign over you will*
> *do: he will take your sons and make them serve with*
> *his chariots and horses… [Others would] … plough*
> *his ground and reap his harvest… he will take your*
> *daughters to be perfumers, cooks and bakers. He will*
> *take the best of your fields and vineyards and olive groves*
> *and give them to his attendants. He will take a tenth of*
> *your grain and of your vintage and give it to his officials*
> *and attendants. Your manservants and maidservants*
> *and the best of your cattle and donkeys he will take for*
> *his own use. He will take a tenth of your flocks and you*
> *yourself will become his slaves. When that day comes*
> *you will cry out for relief from the king you have chosen.*
> (1 Samuel 8:11–18)

Samuel pointed to the fact that in having a king – with all the support and privilege that would be afforded his officials, attendants, and standing army – the level of wastage would be greater than by keeping the nation's governance godly, small, and simple. Having a king would make for a large, unwieldy, expensive, autocratic system that would require much more money, time, energy, and other resources to support. The people would become slaves of this system and the delivery of justice would become a secondary function of government.

Whenever God's blueprint for a governmental system based on truth has been rejected, slavery has been the result.

One of the American founding fathers, Benjamin Franklin, a product of the Puritan movement and part of the Great Enlightenment, stated that, "Only a virtuous people are capable of freedom. As nations become corrupt and vicious, they have more need of masters."[6] To be virtuous means to be morally upright and an adherent to the truth.

As the church, we need to envision and mentor leaders in promoting the virtue of truth in countries that are going backwards. We need to stand in the truth against the corruption and viciousness of the leaders who are leading countries to ruin.

Samuel Adams, brother of John, one of the early US presidents, wrote, "… let us become a virtuous people… if we are universally vicious and debauched in our manners, though the form of our constitution carries the most exalted freedom, we shall in reality be most abject slaves".[7]

Truth is like a river on its journey to the sea. After six weeks canoeing on the Rufiji River, carrying our fire with us, we eventually reached the delta. Here the river braided outwards into many channels as it flowed into the ocean. The river of truth is the same. Out of it flows all the good things of God: righteousness, justice, love, and all the virtues. If the river of truth dries up, then so do the channels that braid out from it.

If the truth is not paramount, the lie takes over. If the lie starts to flow down the river – the lie of greed and the love of money or the quest for power and privilege or the chasing of the lusts of the flesh – all hell breaks loose at the delta with every evil taking place on earth.

The Pharisees were castigated by Jesus:

> *You belong to your father, the devil, and you want*
> *to carry out your father's desire. He was a murderer*
> *from the beginning, not holding to the truth for there*
> *is no truth in him. When he lies he speaks his native*
> *language because he is the father of lies.* (John 8:44)

If we are rooted in truth, we will destroy the lies in our nations with righteousness. Bruce Waltke, the Old Testament scholar says, "The righteous [*tsedeq*] are willing to disadvantage themselves to advantage the community; the wicked are willing to disadvantage the community to advantage themselves."[8]

Peoples, like people, reap what they sow. They cannot escape the eternal truths. Nations that do not first seek the truth always become bonded in slavery. Jesus came to break us out of the slavery of unrighteousness with the truth. After silencing the Sadducees, the Pharisees got together to try to trick him. They asked him, "Which is the greatest commandment in the law?" Jesus replied with the amazing truth about love:

> *Love the Lord your God with all your heart and with all your soul and with all your mind. This is the first and greatest commandment. And the second is like it: Love your neighbour as yourself. All the Law and the Prophets hang on these two commandments.* (Matthew 22:37–40)

The first commandment he took from Deuteronomy 6:4–5, which sums up the first four commandments. Jesus' second command was from Leviticus 19:18, which encapsulates the second six.

The law, as an extension of truth, is a foundational tool of government. Jesus is expounding here a revolutionary truth regarding the essence of law. Love, Jesus tells us, is at the very heart of the law. It is all part of the revolutionary mystery of the truth of grace.

The secular Roman lawyer, Cicero, shed some truth on love and justice too: "For these virtues originate in our natural inclination to love our fellow man and this is the foundation of justice."[9] Aristotle observed that "At his best, man is the noblest of all the animals; separated from law and justice he is the worst."[10]

Laws that reflect truth, born out of an honest love for other people, progress nations. Laws that are born out of self-interest or petty concepts that result in totalitarian control over people's lives suppress the individual and stifle progress. Cicero calls these "pestilential statutes" which "no more deserve to be called laws than the rules a band of robbers might pass in their assembly".[11]

Jesus was the epitome of the truth and love. If the motivating force in our lives does not stem from wanting to promote the truth and love, then the "pestilential statutes" of corrupt governments will continue. How do we enact justice? Job answers, "I put on righteousness as my clothing; justice was my robe and turban" (Job 29:14).

The Frenchman, Alexis de Tocqueville, paid an extensive visit to the United States a generation or so after it became independent. He was so impressed by what he saw that he wrote a definitive book of that time entitled *Democracy in America*. He noted:

> *I sought for the greatness and genius of America in her commodious harbours and her ample rivers, and it was not there; in her fertile fields and boundless prairies, and it was not there; in her rich mines and vast world commerce, and it was not there. Not until I went to the churches of America did I understand the secret of her genius and power. America is great because she is good, and if America ceases to be good, America will cease to be great.[12]*

America was good because it understood the truth. Their constitution, their style of leadership, their commitment to godly laws, justice, and hard work all reflected their active belief in the truth. Within just 129 years of independence, America was the strongest, the most innovative, and the wealthiest nation in the world.

When we, as the church and individual Christians, start the truth revolution, stepping out in confidence for the truth, risking all for the truth, exposing the lies of Satan with the truth, then the truth will begin to flow on its way, carrying its life.

In Proverbs we read that "An honest answer is like a kiss on the lips" (Proverbs 24:26). We must engage in a radical revolution of truth if the "kiss of life" is to indwell us, so that we can stir our nations and pull them back from the brink. The truth revolution must bubble out from our hearts and from our churches, flooding into our families, our schools, our businesses, and ultimately in an overwhelming gush into our governments. The river of the truth revolution must flow, carrying life wherever it goes.

Jesus said: "If you hold to my teaching you are really my disciples. Then you will know the truth and the truth will set you free" (John 8:31–32).

POST SCRIPT

After Mike died as a result of the injuries he sustained during his abduction and torture, we set up the Mike Campbell Foundation as a registered charity in the UK. We still live in Zimbabwe because it is our home and we believe in playing our part to make a future here for the next generation. This is in keeping with Jesus' command to be the "salt" and the "light" in the place that he has put us.

We cannot live on the farm any longer even though Minister Nathan Shamuyarira, who forced us off, is not farming it – and at the age of eighty-five, is unlikely to. After our houses were burnt down with everything in them, the farm continued to be asset-stripped and our former workers are now living without work in penury. The tall, undulating grasses sigh each year until they too are burnt to the ground. No crops are grown or livestock farmed on Mount Carmel any more. Another 1.6 million people are currently surviving on international food aid, but the World Food Program's predicted requirement for 2014 has increased to 2.2 million.

We are doing what we can to teach survival skills to the forgotten farm worker community and bring the message of salvation to them. The few remaining commercial farms continue to be seized without compensation, and the ZANU-PF elite have now started seizing mines and businesses as well. In the wake of the rigged elections of 31 July 2013, President Mugabe's government announced that it planned to seize control of foreign-owned mines without paying for them as part of a programme to accumulate US$7 billion of assets. Such is the insatiable greed of those who continue to abuse their power.

At the same time, the EU, the UK, the US, and Australia are lifting the targeted sanctions against almost all those involved in gross human rights abuses – including Minister Nathan Shamuyarira and the brutal gang leader Gilbert Moyo, who caused the premature death of Mike. There appears to be a concerted agenda from many in the international corridors of power to whitewash the paramount principles of truth and justice in the land of Zimbabwe and to re-engage with Mugabe.

At the time of writing, there remain many uncertainties ahead, but we continue with the fight for truth and justice, and with our efforts to bring in a God-fearing government in the future. We have had the Mugabe government held in contempt of the SADC Tribunal three times, but they have not yet made any move to comply with the law.

As a result of a costs award that the SADC Tribunal gave us, we have registered the judgment in South Africa. The Zimbabwe government appealed after we attached a Zimbabwe government property in Cape Town to pay the legal costs. We won the case in South Africa's Supreme Court of Appeal in September 2010. This was the second high-profile ruling handed down by a South African court against President Mugabe's government. In May 2012, the North Gauteng High Court ruled that South Africa was obliged under international law to arrest the perpetrators of human rights violations in Zimbabwe – should they visit the country.

After the Supreme Court of Appeal ruling, the Zimbabwe government then appealed to South Africa's Constitutional Court, which dismissed its appeal against the Supreme Court's decision. This was an important development in the legal campaign to ensure that Zimbabwe is unable to escape its international law obligations arising from its land seizure programme.

It remains of grave concern that southern Africa's 250 million people can no longer go to the SADC Tribunal when their own justice systems fail them – as they periodically do. This is because, subsequent to our judgment, the SADC Heads of State closed down their internationally respected but increasingly inconvenient regional court. Sadly, Africans will remain in poverty so long as truth and justice are not respected, understood, and championed by fellow Christians and those who appreciate their crucial role in democracy and the rule of law. Africa needs men and women of moral courage, committed to truth and justice if we are to break the bondage and slavery that so many Africans are still subjected to.

An elderly, dispossessed black commercial farmer, Luke Tembani, and I have taken the fourteen SADC Heads of State and their governments to the African Commission on Human and People's Rights for their collective suspension of the SADC Tribunal. Our application asks for an order that will ensure the SADC Tribunal continues to function in all respects as established by Article 16 of the SADC Treaty. It is the first time in legal history that a group of Heads of State and governments has been cited by an individual as the respondent in an application to an international court.

The ACHPR will deliberate on the issue and will pass it on to the African Court, the legal arm of the African Union in Arusha, if it deems that the actions of the SADC Heads of State and their governments are unjustifiable and constitute a violation of the rights of SADC citizens. This is an exciting case and will hopefully go some way to bringing truth and justice to the region.

Though this day may still be some way off, we go forward with hope because we serve a God in whom the final victory is assured. Jesus did not promise that life would not be without its troubles. In fact, he warned, "In this world you will have trouble." But then he said, "Take heart for I have overcome the world!" So we take heart and we go on in that glorious faith knowing that it is not in vain.

One day the golden grasses in Zimbabwe will sing again in truth, instead of sighing and crackling with the consuming fires of wanton destruction. One day I believe the evocative sounds of Africa will harmonize across a peaceful, democratically ruled land that is harvesting its fullness in bounteous blessing.

NOTES

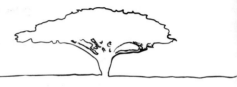

1. A Departure from the Rule of Law and Justice in Zimbabwe

1. Gary Haugen, *Good News About Injustice* (InterVarsity Press, 1999), p. 72.

2. The SADC Tribunal is the highest policy institution of the South African Development Community. In one of its first cases, the Tribunal decided that the Zimbabwean Government may not evict farmer Mike Campbell from his land and that farm evictions per Amendment 17 of Zimbabwe's constitution amounted to de facto discrimination against whites. Following this decision, Zimbabwe pulled out of the SADC Tribunal, challenging its legitimacy.

3. An offer letter is a letter signed by the Minister of Lands offering a certain piece of "acquired" land to a "beneficiary". This piece of paper gives the offer letter holder carte blanche to do what it takes to force the owners of the property out of their home(s) and take – with no compensation – many of their movable assets as well, including tractors, implements, seed, fertilizer and chemicals.

4. Thomas Keneally, *Three Famines* (Random House, Knopf, Australia, 2010).

5. Catholic Commission for Justice and Peace in Zimbabwe and the Legal Resources Foundation, *Breaking the Silence, Building True Peace* (1997). Available at <http://www.archive.org/details/breakingthesilencebuildingtruepeace>

6. ZIPRA: The armed wing of ZAPU was the Chinese-supported Zimbabwe People's Revolutionary Army (ZIPRA), which operated mainly in Matabeleland. ZAPU: The Zimbabwe African People's Union was formed in 1961 with Joshua Nkomo as President, and Robert Mugabe as information and publicity secretary.

7. Available at <http://ww2.unhabitat.org/documents/ZimbabweReport.pdf>

2. What Does God Call Us To Do?

1. "On Forgiveness: A Roundtable Discussion with Jacques Derrida" in John Caputo et al., *Questioning God* (Indiana University Press, 2001), p. 69.

Notes

2. Erwin Lutzer, *Hitler's Cross* (Moody Publishers, 1995), p. 141.

3. Saul Friedlander, *Nazi Germany and the Jews* (Phoenix, 2009), p. 126.

4. From an exhibit by the Federal Ministry of Interior, 1938. *Nazi Rule in Austria* (Austrian Documentation Centre of the Resistance Movement, 1998), p. 15 (translated and abbreviated by Werner Oder).

5. Gonda Redlich, Saul S. Friedman, Laurence Kutler, *The Terezin Diary of Gonda Redlich* (The University Press of Kentucky, 1992).

6. Redlich et al., *Terezin Diary*, pp. 224–25.

7. Die Briefe Pius XII, *An die deutschen Bischöfe 1939–1944* (Mainz, 1966), p. 134.

8. Friedlander, *Nazi Germany and the Jews*, p. 225.

9. Heinrich Portman, *Cardinal Von Galen*, translated by R. L. Sedgwick (Jarrolds, 1957), Third Sermon on 3 August 1941, p. 239–46.

10. Hermann Rauschning, *Hitler Speaks: A Series of Political Conversations with Adolf Hitler on His Real Aims* (T. Butterworth Ltd, 1939).

11. *NewsDay*, 9 November 2010.

12. Operation Murambatsvina (mid-winter 2005): "Operation clean out the filth" or "Drive out the trash" was a massive Zimbabwean government campaign to forcibly bulldoze and destroy homes in cities and towns across the country. Under the guise of a slum-clearance programme, it was widely viewed as a campaign to drive out and make homeless large sections of the urban and rural poor who comprise much of the internal opposition to the Mugabe administration.

13. *The Zimbabwean* newspaper, 2 May 2012.

14. Larry Rasmussen, *Dietrich Bonhoeffer – Reality and Resistance* (Westminster John Knox Press, 2005), p. 68.

15. Eric Metaxas, *Bonhoeffer: Pastor, Martyr, Prophet, Spy – a Righteous Gentile Versus the Third Reich* (Thomas Nelson, 2010).

16. Dietrich Bonhoeffer, *The Cost of Discipleship* (SCM Press, 2001), p. 4.

17. Gary Haugen, *Good News About Injustice* (InterVarsity Press, 1999), p. 90.

18. C. S. Lewis, *The Screwtape Letters* (Collier, 1982).

19. Carl Henry, "A Summons to Justice", *Christianity Today*, 20 July 1992, p. 40.

20. Quoted by Michael Berenbaum, *The World Must Know* (US Holocaust Museum, 1993, 2006), p. 37.

3. How Nations Become Poor and Hungry

1. Ayn Rand, "Man's Rights", from *Capitalism: The Unknown Ideal* (Dutton Signet, 1946). Available at <http://www.aynrand.org/site/PageServer?pagename=arc_ayn_rand_man_rights>

2. Symond Fiske, *Our Principle Problem* (Brevitas, 2002), p. 55.

3. Irving E. Howard, *The Christian Alternative to Socialism* (Better Books, 1966), p. 4.

4. R. J. Rushdoony, *The Bible and Property*. Available at <http://chalcedon.edu/research/articles/the-bible-and-property/>

5. R. J. Rushdoony, *Law and Liberty* (Ross House Books, 2009), p. 83.

6. Calvin Beisner, *Prosperity and Poverty: the Compassionate Use of Resources in a World of Scarcity* (Crossway Books, 1988), p. 66.

7. Udo Middelmann, *Pro-Existence: The Place of Man in the Circle of Existence* (Hodder Christian Paperbacks, 1975), p. 42.

8. "Offering of Uha" (2400 BC) in D. Dunham, *Naga-Ed-Deir Stelae of the First Intermediate Period* (Oxford University Press, 1937), pp. 102–04.

9. G.F Rehmke, "Property Rights and Law Among the Ancient Greeks: The Success of Western Civilization Owes Much to the Greeks", *The Freeman*, 1 February 1997. Available at <http://www.fee.org/the_freeman/detail/property-rights-and-law-among-the-ancient-greeks#ixzz2VKZu6RlO> He quotes from Numa Denis Fustel de Coulanges, *The Ancient City* (Johns Hopkins University Press, 1980 [1864]), pp. 59, 63.

10. Victor Davis Hanson, *The Other Greeks: The Family Farm and the Agrarian Roots of Western Civilization* (The Free Press, 1995), p. 9.

11. While it is true that for much of this period America was still a slave-owning economy, we have to remember that slavery was an established institution worldwide and that at the beginning of the eighteenth century about 75 per cent of the world's population were slaves, so they were dealing with an entrenched position regarding slaves. Despite this, the USA had banned the slave trade by 1808, and Vermont, for example, had already banned slavery by 1777. As far as I know, it is the only country in the world ever to have gone to war in order to do away with slavery altogether.

12. John Locke, *Second Essay Concerning Civil Government*, Ch. 19, Sec. 222.

13. Locke, *Second Essay*, Ch. 11, Sec. 38.

14. Locke, *Second Essay*., Ch. 5, Sec. 27.

15. Quoted by Wesley H. Hillendahl, "Inflation: By-Product of

Ideologies in Collision", *The Freeman* 24, no. 7 (July 1974), p. 415.

16. Quoted by Cleon Skousen, *The 5000 Year Leap* (National Center for Constitutional Studies, 2007), p. 173.

17. Skousen, *The 5000 Year Leap*, p. 173.

18. Charles Francis Adams, *The Works of John Adams*, 10 vols (Little, Brown and Company, 1850–56), Vol. 1, p. 280.

19. Saul K. Padovere (ed.), *The Complete Madison* (Harper and Bros, 1953), p. 267.

20. Dr Ludwig von Mises, *Socialism* (Yale University Press, 1951), p. 583.

4. The Force of Fear and the Power of Love

1. Pungwes are all-night indoctrination meetings that rural communities are forced to attend. At these traumatic events, they are forced to listen to the history of the liberation struggle and to sing "Chimurenga" (war) songs. Individuals are frequently singled out and publicly tortured as an example to the community.

2. Falanga is a method of torture which is used extensively by ZANU-PF and the armed forces. The soles of the feet are beaten with iron rods, logs, or cables. The beatings cause extreme pain at the time of the assault and can cause long-term, irreparable damage, affecting the feet, ankles, and knee joints, and in some cases even damage to the pelvis and lower back. If it is severe, it can be fatal.

5. Godly People Who Overcame Fear and Spoke Truth to Power

1. From a paraphrase of Martin Luther King Jnr's speech during the Great March on Detroit on 23 June 1963.

2. John Calvin, *Commentary on Daniel*, Vol. 1, Lecture XXX.

3. Philip Friedman, *Their Brothers' Keepers* (Holocaust Library, 1978), p. 93.

4. Daniel Goldhagen, *Hitler's Willing Executioners: Ordinary Germans and the Holocaust* (Alfred A. Knopf, 1996), p. 438. According to Genesis 4:9, the answer of Cain was "Am I my brother's keeper?"

5. Goldhagen, *Hitler's Willing Executioners*, p. 437.

6. Arthur C. Cochrane, *The Church's Confession under Hitler* (Westminster Press, 1962), p. 278.

7. William L. Shirer, *The Rise and Fall of the Third Reich* (Secker and Warburg, 1960), pp. 238–39.

8. Geddes MacGregor, *The Thundering Scot* (Westminster Press, 1957).

9. Rene Wind, *Dietrich Bonhoeffer: A Spoke in the Wheel* (Wm. B. Eerdmans, 1991), p. 69.

10. Saul Friedlander, *Nazi Germany and the Jews* (Phoenix, 2009), p. 201.

11. *Time Magazine*, 4 April 1938.

12. *Time Magazine*, 15 December 1941.

13. Friedlander, *Nazi Germany and the Jews*, p. 71.

14. Pinchas Lapide, *Last Three Popes and the Jews* (Souvenir Press, 1967), p. 208.

15. Lapide, *Last Three Popes*, pp. 192–93.

16. Lapide, *Last Three Popes*, p. 36.

17. Lech Wałesa, *A Path of Hope: An Autobiography* (Pan Books, 1987), p. 96.

18. Michael Burleigh, *Sacred Causes: Religion and Politics from the European Dictators to Al Qaeda* (Harper Perennial, 2007), p. 424.

19. Burleigh, *Sacred Causes*, p. 430.

20. A *jambanja* is a state-sponsored, violent confrontation initiated to force farmers and farm workers off the commercial farms. They involve barricading farmers and farm workers into their homes, lighting fires, threats of violence, actual violence, including beatings and sometimes killings. During all-night *jambanjas* or indoctrination sessions, people are forced to sing ZANU-PF songs and to denounce so-called "traitors", usually members or perceived members of the Movement for Democratic Change (MDC) party who are then beaten, sometimes to death. *Jambanjas* can also involve depriving animals of food and water for days on end or even brutalizing them.

6. Jesus and the Law; Injustice and the Authorities

1. *The Teddy Bear's Picnic* is a song consisting of a melody by American composer John Walter Bratton, written in 1907, and lyrics added by Irish sonwriter Jimmy Kennedy in 1932.

7. Pulling the Christian Thread Through History

1. G. M. Trevelyan, *English Social History* (Prentice Hall Press, 1965).

2. Trevelyan, *English Social History*.

3. Danny Danziger and John Gillingham, *1215: The Year of the Magna Carta* (Coronet, 2004), p. 278.

4. Václav Havel, Speech at the International Symposium on Master Jan Hus, Vatican, 17 December 1999.

5. Professor Montagu Burrows, 1881 lecture series "Wycliffe's Place in History" as quoted in *Christianity Today International Magazine*, Issue 3, 1983.

6. John Dalrymple, *Memoirs of Great Britain and Ireland; from the Dissolution of the Last Parliament of Charles the Second Till the Capture of the French and Spanish Fleets at Vigo* (London, 1790).

8. Rising Faith, Turning Tyranny: Sparks of Hope

1. Augustine of Hippo, *De Libero Arbitrio* [On Free Will].

2. John Calvin, *Institutes of the Christian Religion*, IV.XX.32, "Of Civil Government: Obedience due only in so far as compatible with the word of God".

3. Jonathan Mayhew, *A Discourse Concerning Unlimited Submission and Non-Resistance to the Higher Powers* (Boston, 1750). Available at <http://digitalcommons.unl.edu/etas/44/>

4. Michael Burleigh, *Sacred Causes: Religion and Politics from the European Dictators to Al Qaeda* (Harper Perennial, 2007), p. 155.

5. Francis A. Schaeffer, *The Complete Works of Francis A. Schaeffer: A Christian Worldview* (Crossway Books, 1988), p. 468.

6. John Stott, *The Message of Romans: God's Good News for the World* (Inter Varsity Press, 1994), p. 342.

7. John Stott Ministries, 10 October 2001.

8. Steve Camp, *Corporate Worship in the Church? Chevrolet and the Word of God, an Open Letter to the Contemporary Christian Music Community*. Available at <http://stevenjcamp.blogspot.co.uk/2005/07/chevrolet-presents-come-together-and.html>

9. John Stott Ministries.

10. Robert Moffat, *The Matabele Journals of Robert Moffat 1829–1860* (National Archives of Rhodesia, 1976).

11. Moffat, *Matabele Journals*.

12. Moffat, *Matabele Journals*.

13. Moffat, *Matabele Journals*.

14. Rob Mackenzie, *David Livingstone: The Truth Behind the Legend*, ninth edition (Zimbabwe: Figtree Publications, 2007), p. 70.

15. Scott A. Beaulier, *Explaining Botswana's Success: The Critical Role of Post-Colonial Policy* (CATO Institute, 2003), pp. 234–37.

16. IMF in 2011 – GDP per capita at purchasing power parity.

17. Roger Scruton, *Is Democracy Over-rated?*, BBC Radio 4, 11 August 2013.

18. *New York Times*, 28 August 2004.

19. Maggie Kriel, circular email entitled *Prayers for Peace*, 6 June 2003.

20. BBC interview, December 2003.

21. *New York Times*, 28 August 2004.

22. Sokwanele Report, *Witness to the Nation*, 25 March 2005.

23. *VOA News*, 26 June 2006.

24. Revd Graham Shaw, Tribute to Archbishop Pius Ncube, 9 February 2013.

25. Revd Noel Scott, Tribute to Archbishop Pius Ncube, 12 February 2013.

26. Fr Nigel Johnson SJ, Tribute to Archbishop Pius Ncube, 17 February 2013.

27. PBS Frontline/World, 27 June 2006.

28. Shaw, Tribute.

9. The Truth Will Set You Free!

1. Symond Fiske, *Our Principle Problem* (Brevitas, 2002), p. 63.

2. Fiske, *Our Principle Problem*, p. 173.

3. Quoted by Fiske, *Our Principle Problem*, p. 104.

4. The Marshall Plan was a plan conceived by the USA for rebuilding the allied countries of Europe after the Second World War.

5. Martin Meredith, *The State of Africa: A History of the Continent Since Independence* (Simon and Schuster, 2011), p. 379.

6. Albert Henry Smyth, *The Writings of Benjamin Franklin*, Vol. 9 (Ulan Press, 2012), p. 569.

7. William V. Wells, *The Life and Public Services of Samuel Adams*, Vol. 1 (HardPress, 2008), pp. 22–23.

8. Quoted by Raymond C. Ortlund Jnr, *Proverbs: Wisdom That Works* (Crossway Books, 2012), p. 177.

9. William Ebenstein, *Great Political Thinkers: from Plato to the present* (Wadsworth Publishing Co. Inc., 1999), p. 134.

10. *Complete Works of Aristotle* (Berlin: Prussian Academy of Sciences, 1831–1870), Bekker Number Book 1, 1253.a 31.

11. Ebenstein, *Great Political Thinkers*, pp. 134–35.

12. Cleon Scousen, *The 5000 Year Leap* (National Center for Constitutional Studies, 2006), p. 84.

INDEX

Index

Index